The
Ghost
Who
Would
Not
Die

Also by Linda Alice Dewey

Aaron's Crossing

The Ghost Who Would Not Die

A Runaway Slave
A Brutal Murder
A Mysterious Haunting

10-3-08

LINDA ALICE DEWEY

Linda Alice Dewey

HAMPTON ROADS
PUBLISHING COMPANY, INC.

Cover design by Jane Hagaman
Cover art: *Tombstones in a Cemetary* © by [Svante Hultquist] / [Nordic
Photos] / Getty Images; *Young Man with Eyes Closed* © by [Thomas
Barwick] / [Riser] / Getty Images

Hampton Roads Publishing Company, Inc.
1125 Stoney Ridge Road
Charlottesville, VA 22902

434-296-2772
fax: 434-296-5096
email: hrpc@hrpub.com
www.hrpub.com

If you are unable to order this book from your local
bookseller, you may order directly from the publisher.
Call 1-800-766-8009, toll-free.

Library of Congress Cataloging-in-Publication Data

Jacobs (Spirit)
  The ghost who would not die : a runaway slave, a brutal murder, a
mysterious haunting / Linda Alice Dewey.
      p. cm.
  Summary: "Jacobs was a Civil War-era slave who was brutally murdered. In
the present day, the author meets Jacobs's ghost and learns the story of his
life as a slave, a runaway, and a vagrant in nineteenth-century
America"--Provided by publisher.
  ISBN 978-1-57174-585-9 (tp : alk. paper)
  1. Spirit writings. I. Dewey, Linda Alice. II. Title.
  BF1301.J14 2008
  133.1--dc22
                                2008020710

ISBN 978-1-57174-585-9
10 9 8 7 6 5 4 3 2 1
Printed on acid-free paper in Canada

Author's Note

This book is a work of creative nonfiction. The events involving the author actually took place. The other events may have. Some names and places have been changed to protect the privacy of those still living. The author of this book does not advise ghost hunting or ghost busting. The author's intent is simply to offer information that may help you on your own path through life towards spiritual and emotional well-being. Should you choose to use any of the information in this book on your path—which is your right—the author and publisher assume no responsibility for your actions.

To Todd, who helped me market the last one
To Evan, who started me off on this one

TABLE
OF
CONTENTS

ACKNOWLEDGMENTS

In October 2006, Jack Jennings, CEO of Hampton Roads Publishing, asked me what I'd been working on since *Aaron's Crossing*. I told him I was helping my father write his book about his World War II experience in a disastrous air battle known as the Kassel Mission.

"I'm also working on a book about the ghost I helped after Aaron," I said. "He was a runaway slave during the Civil War, with a twisted foot and his name was Jacobs with an *s*." I laughed. The idea was outrageous. Who would make *that* up?

Immediately enthusiastic, Jack put in for Hampton Roads to publish the book and they sent me a contract. Since it was scheduled to come out in Fall 2008, I put Dad's book aside. At eighty-four, he was healthy and we already had the chapters about the mission covered. I went right to work on Jacobs's story. Writing rolled along smoothly through the winter and I finished the first draft at the end of January 2007. Of course, the first draft is the quickest part of writing a book. It's also the scariest because, the way I write, I never know what's going to happen in the story.

On March 25, 2007, I received a call at 5 a.m. Dad had died of a heart attack. It took months for me to get back to Jacobs's story. You can imagine my regret and self-recrimination. No longer was Dad there to finish dictating his story to me. But wait. We could still do it. He'd just have to dictate to me from the Other Side. Though this may have been obvious, getting past the regret was still a process. I listened for Dad and received messages for Mom and myself. I could do it. One day, I would finish his book.

Back to work on Jacobs's story, the next bump came in September—back surgery. Bob Friedman at Hampton Roads expressed nothing but concern that I get well. The book could wait.

I recuperated faster than normal and finished editing the book in four months—record time for me, but a year after completing the first draft.

And so I wish to thank my father for his sacrifice; my mother for her amazing strength; Jack Jennings and Bob Friedman for their foresight and patience; all the supportive people at Hampton Roads and in my life; my many "first readers" who dropped everything when it came time to read the manuscript; and everyone in this story.

Most of all, I thank God for gifts we constantly receive, and Jacobs, who continually reminded me that I wasn't the one writing this book.

"Miss," he'd say when I got stuck, "you done forgot all about how to do this now, didn't you? Just listen and glide along."

He was right. That's all we have to do.

Linda Alice Dewey
January 20, 2008
Martin Luther King Weekend

PROLOGUE

MICHIGAN 2003

In doing our best, we break the bonds of our
own slavery and proclaim freedom for all.
—Author's Journal, February 2008

Evan saw him first.

"Mom, we're not alone," he said.

"Honey, of course we're not alone." I didn't even look up from my work. "God's always—"

"No, Mom, we're not alone in this *house.*"

I turned to him. "What do you mean?"

"Last night while you were gone, I used your microphone to rap with a CD. I was looking at myself in the picture window, like this." He rapped out the words to a song while he watched his reflection in the window bounce. He had the moves down.

I tried not to smile.

"Then I went like this." Feet planted, he twisted and bounced to the side then back to center. "I thought I saw something, so I did it again." He bounced left a second time, then stopped. "It was still there."

"What was?"

"A black shape, Mom. It didn't move. "

A black shape?

"We're not alone."

Ghosts don't have black shapes, do they?

"Were you scared?" I asked.

"I quit and went up to my room."

"Did you see it after that?"

"No, but it's still here."

"How do you know?"

"I can feel it."

Sometimes you have to see something yourself, like I did years before, to understand. Now that he'd seen one, Evan knew.

I knew what I had to do. Sitting down at my computer, I said a prayer to be clear and listened telepathically for the voice of this new ghost. I typed what I heard, printed it out, and handed it to Evan, who sat on the couch.

When he finished reading, he looked up. His beautiful sixteen-year-old face, which knew too well how to mask feeling, over-flowed with emotion. "It's him."

"How can you tell?"

"I just know."

I looked at this ghost's story. Could I help him by myself? The only other time I'd helped a ghost cross over, I was there when he crossed and knew it was real, just like Evan felt this ghost with us now. But when it came right down to it, all I had really done was give moral support. Was what I was thinking even possible?

The next morning, I did help this ghost cross to the Other Side. Unsure of how to do it, I lit a few candles, closed my eyes and said a prayer, then went into a light meditation. I asked for help from above and that this one be allowed to cross over to what you might call "Heaven."

I concentrated my energy, pushing upwards, then out-wards—like parting the Red Sea. I would later learn that all I had to do was ask for this to be done. But now, it seemed in my meditation that the ceiling opened and the skies above it. And then, he just floated up until I could no longer feel him near.

The skies and ceiling closed, and it felt lighter, clearer, in the room.

He was the first I ever crossed over all by myself. But I shouldn't have.

Three years later, I wondered if I could connect with him, so I checked in to see how he was and what had happened since our encounter. What follows in this book is what he told me.

Taking down this story wasn't easy. Self-doubt lurked every time I turned on the computer. Sure, I had done this before—once. Could I do it again? Then Jacobs would remind me to relax. The words would flow and off we'd go as I let Jacobs's story wend its way through my mind and onto the page. He often answered my questions or doubts before they even had a chance to surface.

Once, as I typed, I grew suspicious. Did I really hear him talk to me? If so, how much of it was me, and how much him? Did I influence it?

This was his answer:

> Yes, I hear your thoughts as we work together, Miss. Helps me understand what you need to know. I try to answer in my story so you get things from your way of seeing. But every once in a while, your thinking pesters me to say something so you can understand.
>
> It takes the two of us to get this done, and I'm not just a-talking about me dictating and you taking it down. I'm talking about our thinking interlapping—no, interweaving—to make this more complete. Couldn't be no other way now, could it?

I couldn't imagine a runaway slave saying words like "interweaving." He addressed his reply to the reader:

> When you read this book, you'll wonder at how I talk so good sometimes and sometimes not. You gots to understand something. Even though I was born and raised a slave, I got me an education in my own way. So when you see odd words here and there, that's one reason.

Another is that this-here story comes through this lady. Sometimes her mind changes my words but not often. Most of the time when something don't sound right, we have a little to-and-fro over it, her and me.

Another time, when I bucked again at his choice of words, he stopped what he was saying to interject:

My big words bothering you again, ma'am? I'm not the soul I was, no, ma'am. In fact, there ain't no color here where I am now, no country of origin either. I done linked up with my "Super-Soul," if you want to call it that. I'm identifying with my life as Jacobs right now cause that's how I came to be with you, ma'am, so that's who I sound like now. But I'm so much more than that.

You'll see some of your lingo here, since this all comes through you. But you'll also see my own terms that come from other ways of being, other places, other identities. We each are so much more than we think we are. And we're susceptible to others' ways of thinking too, without being aware of it. Yes, ma'am, susceptible. That's a big word too, now isn't it?

He didn't mean "Super-Soul," I thought.

You want to call it your "Oversoul"? He answered. *Go right ahead.*

For all his lapses in linguistic consistency, Jacobs's story of the struggle for freedom from outer—as well as inner—slavery is worth telling. May we all have such a story to tell at the end of our time on this beautiful blue-green planet.

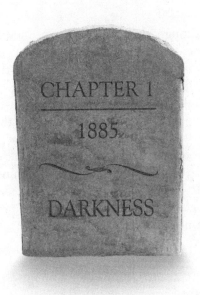

CHAPTER 1

1885

DARKNESS

I feel I owe it to those left behind to let you know what you got to look forward to if you don't tend to yourself where you are right now.
—J. Johnson

You never know what's gonna happen when you die till you get there. For some, it's a smooth ride. For others, it's a dark tunnel to the White Light. For someone like me, it was an empty corner of the universe.

Now, I don't want to scare nobody. You gots to know things will all work out. It's just that sometimes you gotta wait for the good ending.

For me, one minute I'm a-saying goodbye to the stars, and the next I'm a-floating in a sea of nothing. Wasn't dark, wasn't light. More like what you see on a cloudy day with a bit of a glow. I could move my arms and legs, but there wasn't no place to go and nothing to do—not even to scratch myself, cause I didn't itch. I could feel my outsides all right, yes I could. And I was still in my clothes.

At first, I thought it was a dream I couldn't get out of. Know how some dreams seem so real? Like you wake up but you're still dreaming? This was even more real than that.

In dreams, though, something's always going on. Here, with no sun to tell me the time and no clocks a-ticking, I can't tell you how long it took me finally to believe that this was, in fact, real. And it was just me here. Nothing else. Nobody else. Just me, wide-awake, hanging around in this-here Space.

After a while, The Space got to be like a thing to me, and I started talking to it like it was separate from me.

"So, what's going on?" I asked The Space.

Course, nothing answered.

"Hey!"

Nothing.

"HEY!!!"

Nothing again.

I floated around for I-don't-know-how-long and got fidgety and restless.

Still, nothing happened.

I closed my eyes, thoughts rolling around inside my head, like, *Maybe I'm lost.*

When you lose something, you go over what you were doing just before you lost it. Well, I started going over what I done just before I got here. . . .

Me and Old Tom, it was, over by the railroad tracks. A train rumbling by . . .

My thoughts came back to this Space. *It's so damned quiet,* I thought. *No sounds except for ones I make. No smells either. Weird. This place is weird.*

I FORGOT!

I just plum forgot a whole space of time between saying goodbye to the stars and waking up in this-here Space!

Like a dream coming back, bits and pieces return to my memory. Someone running, footsteps fading, a train whistle.

Raising my dizzy head, I see . . .

Darkness. Darkness all around, like looking through black glass. I remember now. Through that darkness, I seen Old Tom in the distance, running for all get-out. Dark firelight—trash burning in the railroad yard. I couldn't really see the street lamp over this way too good. Everything was so dark!

Maybe I hit my head when I fell. Or maybe . . . I touched my eyes, then looked at my hands. I could hardly see them.

My spectacles! They must have gotten knocked off in the fight. Where were they? I looked all around me. *Oh Lordy, what will I do without my spectacles?*

I looked up at the sky. Where were the stars? I used to be able to see them without my spectacles. Now I couldn't see them at all.

Oh, Mama, I'm going blind!

I got up real careful and limped back to the camp to find my woman. She'd help me. Then I remembered I didn't have a woman no more. In fact, I'd been getting together with Old Tom's woman. That's how this whole thing started.

Who could I go to for help?

Old Mammy. She loved everybody and everybody loved her. Through the darkness, I hitched off to her shack, rolling past tents and tarpaulins. There she sat like always, on a stool in front of her place, a-talking to a neighbor lady. Old Mammy didn't get around too good. Her frame just couldn't take her bulk no more, but she was laughing as usual.

"Geraldine! You got to be funning me."

Pulling myself to her, I cried out, "Mammy!"

Skinny old Geraldine sitting next to Mammy, laughed right along with her. "I tell you, every word's the truth!"

"Mammy," I said, "I'm going blind!"

Geraldine and Old Mammy watched the shenanigans over by the warming fire. Suddenly, their faces screwed up in pain.

"Wonder what was in that supper Joe fixed tonight," Mammy said, rubbing her belly. "It ain't setting all that well."

"Owww!" wailed Geraldine as she rubbed the back of her neck. She looked at Mammy and said, "Can bad food hurt your neck?"

They slapped their knees and laughed again.

My eyes fixed on the fire—it was so dark! "My eyes, my eyes!" I howled, rubbing them. Again I looked at the fire, but it was still dark.

"Don't know about them two," said Geraldine, nodding at a couple sitting by the fire, their backs to us, his arm across her shoulders. Dark firelight flickered on their faces as they turned to each other.

"Me neither," said Old Mammy, shaking her head at the couple. "Mm, mm, mmm!"

"He too young for her."

I knelt in front of Mammy and put my hands on her knees. "Mammy! For God's sake, look at me!"

"My goodness!" Mammy put her hands on her belly. "I'm a-hurting tonight."

Geraldine looked her up and down. "Girl, ain't you done childbearing?"

They broke up all over again, then went back to holding in their aches and pains.

"Well," Mammy sighed, standing, "I better get to bed. It's been a long day."

I reached out to her, but then the most awful thing happened. I fell right through her to the ground! In shock, I rolled onto my back and looked up at the two women.

Geraldine was up and walking away. "'Night," she said with a lazy smile, still massaging her neck.

"Good night." Old Mammy held her belly with one hand and shut her door with the other, leaving me looking up at stars I couldn't see.

"Good night," I said and closed my eyes.

I opened them to see a group of people looking at me real funny. A dark shape—maybe air—surrounded each.

"He's one of us, all right," said a big white man.

"I . . . I can't hardly see," I said.

"Then you'se one of us for sure," said a black woman with a cloud around her so dark there was no telling where it ended and she began.

"You ain't going blind, if that's what you're wondering," whispered an old white man in overalls. "We all think that at first."

Looking from one to the other, I asked, "Who are you?"

"We're Shadows," said the big woman. "That's what they call us. You got one around you too."

"Why's everything so dark?"

In an instant, she got real mad. "I done told you," she spat. "Looking through your shadow makes everything darker."

"Then my eyes—they're all right?"

The farmer in overalls coughed. "Well," he said, "there ain't nothing about you that's all right."

I stood. "What do you mean?"

The big white man spoke up. "You ain't really a person no more. You're a Shadow now, like us."

"You're people. You all got something strange going on around you, but you're people. I can see that much."

"Well," said the farmer, "you coming or not?"

"Wait a minute," said I. "Are you telling me I can't see, cause I got black around me like you-all?"

I held out my arm. The air close to it was real dark, then faded a foot or so away. Moving my arm up, the dark shape curved in along my body and moved with my arm, like a shirt stretching for me to get into it.

A kid with blond hair down to his eyebrows shook his head. "You got a lot to learn. Come on," he said to the others.

They moved off.

"Hey," I called, but they were gone.

Butter Ned and Sammie—the couple by the fire—leaned against each other, drunk as all get-out as they lurched towards me now.

Butter Ned mumbled something under his breath and laughed.

Sammie giggled. "Shhhh," she warned. But she tripped and screeched as she lost her balance. Butter Ned tried to grab her, missed, and laughed as she stumbled, heading right for me. I tried to get out of the way, but she fell right through me just like I went through Old Mammy! I didn't feel it then and I didn't feel it now.

Squealing, Sammie pushed herself off Mammy's shack and back up through me. Reeling, she said, "Shee-it. I better get to bed."

He gave her a nasty smile. "We getting there, girl."

Their laughter died away. Then it was just me sitting there again.

Folks I never seen before stayed at the fire all night, drinking and carousing so loud you'd think Old Mammy would yell at them to shut up. But she didn't and they didn't.

What with the noise outside and the spinning inside my head, I didn't get no sleep at all. Just before dawn, the bandits I used to hang out with returned, their loot under their coats. They skulked by without a "hey" or a "hi"—like they didn't see me. Cause they couldn't.

They couldn't see me.

I spent a long time thinking about that and the ones that could see me. "Shadows," they called us. What did it mean anyway—all this darkness around me? If I wasn't blind, what was I?

Morning came and still I sat by Old Mammy's shack. With daylight, the darkness around me showed up even better. When I looked down at my hands or body or held out my arm, the cloud looked darker than everywhere else. It wasn't my eyes after all. They were right—I looked through a darkness that stuck to me.

I had a whole lot of new questions. Did this-here darkness keep people from seeing me? How could Sammie fall through me, and me fall through Old Mammy? Answers I didn't want waited, but I was bound to stay blind to them long as I could.

Doors opened. Tent flaps flipped up. Women carried slop to the river. Men threw logs on the fire. Fish sizzled.

Behind me, Mammy's door opened. Poking her head out, she sniffed, then smiled—eyes closed, soaking in the scent. "Mmm-MM! Sure do smell good!"

"I don't smell nothing," I muttered.

Her eyes clouded over. She put her hand to her belly and closed the door.

Geraldine's door flew open and her skimpy shape dashed through it. "Who caught fish and didn't tell me?" She thought herself the best fish-fryer around. "Queen of the Fry," I used to call her.

Everybody except me headed to the fire.

You-all don't even know I'm here, I thought.

A shout over by the train tracks. More calls, then a scream. A rush to see what it was. I got up and limped over behind them. The crowd was so thick, I had to stand on my tippy-toes and stretch to see. Up I went, moving above—no, over—them. And then I seen what all the excitement was about.

Jesus. It was me down there on the ground, a big old stab wound under my ribs, blood everywhere, my open eyes looking up at . . . at me!

Oh Lordy, Lordy, Lordy. I floated above, weeping and staring at my dead face down below.

"I was a-looking at the stars . . . ," I said, dazed. "Last thing them eyes seen. . . ." I touched the eyes I had now. I couldn't cotton it. "If them's my eyes down there, what am I seeing with now?" I asked. My arms and legs flailed around above the mob. "What are these?" Sailing above the crowd as they carried my body back to the camp, I pointed to the body I wore now and asked, "What is this?"

What am I? is a question I didn't want to ask.

Back at Old Mammy's, I sat down but felt out of place. *If I had my own home, I'd go there,* I thought. I used to laugh about it with the fellow I bunked with that first year.

"Why do I need a place? I got one with my woman."

"Yep," laughed Joe. "And when you're done with that one, what you gonna do?"

"Find me another," I said. "I got nothing to worry about."

Now I wished I had a home of my own.

"You don't need a home." A little girl sitting next to me jolted me out of my doldrums—pretty little thing, her hair all done up in pigtails.

"Who are you?" I asked.

"Jessie."

"Jessie who?" When she didn't answer, I looked hard at her. "I don't remember seeing you round here."

"I was here before you."

"What you talking about?" I looked at her real good now—pinafore over an old dress, everything dirty. Couldn't be older than eleven at most. I tried to count back the winters. . . .

"I remember the day you got here."

Pointing to the ground, I asked, "Here?"

"To this-here camp." She smiled. "You were so happy to find a place filled with folk just like you."

This was craziness. "You ain't old enough to remember that."

"Oh, I remember," she smiled. "You wore a dirty old blue shirt, brown pants, and black shoes. And you had a big old straw hat on your head."

I nearly forgot. They gave me them clothes at the nun's house. "How you know that?"

"Seen you come in," she said.

"Honey, you weren't even born then. Your mama tell you that?"

"My mama didn't tell me nothing 'bout it. Seen it myself."

Something else came to my mind. "How . . . how come you're talking to me?"

She got up to go. "I . . . I thought you wanted company."

"I do!" I took her hand. "Honey-child, you can see me? And hear me?"

"I'm talking to you, ain't I?"

I tightened my grip on her little hand, looking at it. *I'm holding her hand!* "But honey, how come *you* can see me and—"

She tried to pull away.

I dropped her hand. "Sorry."

She closed her eyes and passed her hand across her forehead. "I . . . I don't feel so good."

I studied her further. "You're the first person I been able to touch since . . . since . . ."

"Since you died?"

I stood. "You know for sure that I'm dead?"

"Yep," she nodded, then pointed to Old Tom coming our way with Nancy. "That man, he done it."

Flash of Old Tom when he came into his tent unexpected, me and Nancy covering ourselves, her voice cutting through the night. "You supposed to be out looting."

"Guess you thought wrong," he said, and came at me, but I got away.

Now I looked down at this little thing next to me. "How you know all this?"

"Seen it," she answered.

"You seen the fight?"

"Seen him chase and fight and kill you."

"How come you weren't home, asleep in your bed?"

"Can't sleep."

I shook my head. "Your mama let you prowl and spy on people at night?"

"Mama don't know I'm around."

"What? Why not?"

"Cause I'm dead like you."

CHAPTER 2

1885

NIGHTMARE

There's a time for me and a time for you and for all God's children.
—J. Johnson

We watched the others clean up around the fire, then scatter to their homes. A few with nothing better to do stayed to chat.

Got me to thinking. "Say," I said, "you see them folks round the fire last night after everybody went off to sleep?"

She sniffed. "Oh, them? They got nothing better to do."

"Who are they? I never seen them before."

"Oh," she said, "they're sort of like you and me."

"You mean . . . they're dead too?"

"Yeah." She thought a moment. "They're more like me than you, though."

I had so many questions. "You talk to them?"

"A little, but they ain't interested in children."

"How you know that?"

"If they liked kids, they'd have some."

"But you could ask them for help."

She turned, her face a blank. "Now how they gonna help me?"

What would make a little thing like this be so empty, like she had no insides?

"I don't know. Maybe they could tell you what to do."

She laughed, without smiling. "What they gonna say? Turn left at the next corner and you'll be home?"

I didn't know what I was talking about. Even if the place looked the same, it was a whole new sit-yation. "So. What are we supposed to do?"

"Do?" She smiled a smile too old for this little girl. "There ain't nothing to do."

"So we just wait?"

"Wait for what? Ain't nothing gonna happen."

"What you mean? Don't they come and, like, take you across or something?"

"Who?" she asked. "Who's gonna do that?"

I looked around, then shrugged. "I don't know. Angels or something. Somebody."

She stood up and stretched. "Nah," she said in the middle of a yawn, then cringed and held her tummy. "Nobody comes here except folks like the ones that stopped by to see you last night. And them folks round the fire. They're here a lot." She waved. "See you later."

Lying back against Mammy's shed, I said, "Think I'll take a little nap."

"Good luck with that." She disappeared down the path and into the woods.

Dreaming, I floated up and away from the shanty, from the town, from the city—up and out towards the stars till there was nothing but glowing green emptiness all around me.

Jerking awake, I opened my eyes and looked up at a pitch-black night. Mammy's shed sagged behind me. The fire crackled and popped over there. Sitting up, I remembered the little girl, Jessie. Mammy smelling the fish cooking. Sammie falling through me, me falling through Mammy, them people at the fire.

I wished little Jessie was here so I could ask her more questions. She said them folks by the fire were more like her than me. What did she mean? Did she know about them Shadow folks? Did they invite her to go with them like they did me? Where did she go when she left? What did they do with my body? I lost track of it after they carried it back to camp. They must have buried it at some cemetery.

Out of the blue, she stood in front of me, pointing west. "It's over there. Nobody ever visits, but that's where they bury everybody," she said and shuffled away.

In the short time I'd been awake, it had turned from pitch black to daylight. People milled everywhere. How did that happen? Usually you watch the sun come up, thinking your thoughts, but I'd been thinking my thoughts without seeing the change. It might have been daytime but everything was dark like yesterday. Sounds seemed more far-off too.

Jessie passed by, going down to the fire. I got up to follow her.

"Morning," she said from behind me, scuffling by a second time.

But she was just . . .

"Wait!" I yelled.

She stopped.

"I just seen you go by, and now you're going by again in the same direction."

She nodded. "Uh-huh."

"But you didn't come back and turn around."

She started walking to the fire.

"Hey!" I called. I ran up, blocking her way. "Hold it!"

She stopped.

"How'd you do that?"

"What?"

"Go past me and then pass me again without coming back."

"Oh. Hmmm . . ." Her eyes looked distant, then back at me. "I don't know." She left me standing mid-path. I hurried to catch up.

"You just did it yourself," she said.

"Did what?"

"Jumped ahead. You wanted to catch up to me so you jumped ahead."

"Child, I don't know what you're talking about."

She stopped. "Think about it. You jumped time."

"What?"

"You'll get used to it." She disappeared.

I sat down by the fire, muttering. "What the hell's going on? 'Jumping time'?"

"No time like the present," said old Horace, sitting on a stump the other side of the fire. Horace had to be seventy-five years of age if he was a day. Couldn't see or hear diddly. Carried on his own conversation from sunup till sundown—at least we all *thought* he was talking with hisself.

Now I looked over at him. "Hey, Horace."

"Hey, yourself," said blind old Horace who never answered nobody. He spoke awful low though. I could hardly hear him.

"Hey, Horace," I repeated.

"Hey, yourself," he said again.

Christ Almighty! He couldn't hear people, but he could hear me! "How you doing?"

"Not bad," he answered. "A little achy just now, but I ain't complaining."

I smiled. "An ache in your joints, huh, Horace?"

"Yes, sir. Some days worse than others."

I laughed. "Horace, you can hear me."

"Course I hear you," he said. "Can see you too."

"All them conversations you have, Horace—you been talking to folks like me!" I laughed again. "Ain't that the strangest."

He sipped his coffee. "They think I'm crazy. I can't help if they don't talk loud enough or if my old eyes don't work like theirs. But some things I see and hear real good that they don't." Setting his cup down, he said, "I don't argue. Let them think what they will. It don't change things none."

Two of the night bandits approached the fire, listening to Horace as they poured themselves coffee.

"Crazy Horace," said one, with a toothless smile.

Horace chatted with me. "Yeah, this here's an achy day."

I moved across and sat down next to him.

Horace winced and rubbed his stomach. "Damn." He looked at his cup. "Must be this coffee."

"So, Horace, all this time you been talking with people the rest of us couldn't see? But they were real?"

"Course they were real. You're real, ain't ya?"

The other bandit shook his head. "Crazy old coot." He yawned. "I gotta get me some shut-eye." They turned and walked off. "We done real good last night. . . ."

"Many others like me around here?" I asked Horace.

The sun glinted off yellow teeth as Horace laughed and waved towards the woods. "Here comes another one now."

A figure made its way to the fire—bent head covered with an old-fashioned cap, clothes tattered and worn. He wore spectacles like mine and sported a beard but no mustache. His belly hung over trousers held up by suspenders. Looked like he could have used a good night's sleep, like me. He eyed a tin mug in the dirt, wiped it clean, poured hisself a cup of coffee, and sat down. My guess is anybody watching would see that cup and coffeepot doing a little dance as the coffee made its way from one to the other.

Mighty interesting to see him drink it all down just like regular folk. I would soon learn that ghosts eat and drink if they want. Don't know where it all goes, cause you sure don't see it again once it's on your insides. Don't feel it neither. Most don't even taste it. Don't know why they do it at all, but there you have it.

"How you doing this morning?" asked Horace.

Fella just stared at the fire.

Horace grunted. "He ain't much for talking. Not like some of the others."

I thought about the Shadow People and the night-fire folks.

"Most come when everyone else is gone. They figure it's their turn at the fire."

"Must be the ones I seen the other night," I said.

"Could be. They're a crazy lot."

"Made such a racket, I couldn't sleep."

"From what I hear," said Horace, "sleep don't come easy to you folks."

You folks? And how come he could see us when nobody else could?

"Little girl came to visit me," I told Horace.

"Jessie?"

"You know her?" I asked.

"Yep. A fine girl. Too bad about her mama."

"Why? What happened?"

"Her gentleman wouldn't give her the time of day once he found out she was with child, so she came here to have her baby and live. Little Jessie died of the fever when she was near seven. Her mama ain't been the same since—pining for her baby, pining for her man. You never met Sally?"

I shook my head.

He pointed to a lone tent in a meadow near the forest. "Lives over there."

I looked. There in the center of the field stood little Jessie, watching the tent from a distance.

"Girl never leaves her mama. Surprised she came to see you."

Such a nice little girl. "Why does she stay there?"

"Where's she gonna go? This is her home. That's her mama, the one she loves."

"So," I said, "people die and just stay round?"

"Some do. Some don't."

"What happens to the ones that don't?"

Horace sat back and sighed. His face screwed up in pain again, then cleared. "I ain't seen it but once or twice. They just sort of up and . . . disappear."

He looked at me. "You one of them dark ones." He shook his head. "Nasty fight you had the other night. They caught him, you know."

I sat up. "Old Tom?"

"Yep. Somebody seen him run off the night it happened. Didn't think much of it till they found your body yesterday and put two and two together."

His voice faded off, though he still talked. In fact, all the sounds—the crackle of the fire, birds singing, wind blowing the leaves—faded off for a minute. Then it all came back.

"Caught him when he snuck back in to pack up. Took him to the po-lice." He flinched and massaged his neck.

"How's . . . how's . . ."

"Your woman? Nancy ain't happy. With Tom arrested and you gone, she ain't got nobody at all."

Little Nancy, with the sway in her walk and them fetching eyes. Her chesty laugh. I couldn't resist her and, when you think about it, that's what killed me. Ha! Something I couldn't resist killed me.

The other ghost, the silent one from the woods, smiled. "You got that right."

"What?" I asked.

"What you can't resist kills ya."

I stood. "How do you know what I . . ."

"Nothing." He got up and emptied his cup into the fire, set it back where he had found it, then turned to leave.

I got in his face. "Wait a minute."

He smiled again but not with his eyes. "You learn quick."

"What you talking about?"

"You jumped here." He swayed and closed his eyes. "Whew. Dizzy."

He was right. One minute I stood up. The next, I was in front of him.

I must have looked surprised, cause he laughed and shook his head. "You don't know what you're doing yet, do you?" He walked off and, in a flash, disappeared into the woods.

Old Horace rose, stood next to me, and emptied his cup into the fire too. "I'll leave you to your thoughts. You got a lot of sorting to do."

I watched him go, then looked around, coming back to my first question. *Why is everything so dark? And so quiet?*

Evening came, but I hadn't moved—going through the past day or two, trying to catch the strangeness, working on what was different. *And look at me now,* I thought, suddenly aware. How I could stay in this one spot like a statue for so long gave me even more to chew on. From the feel of it, I could stand here till Kingdom Come.

I turned to the fire. Them loud night-people raising hell again, but not as loud as the night before. No crickets chirped either. I could feel a breeze, but couldn't hear it rustle the trees. I looked to the forest, thinking maybe a quiet spot might await my weary head. As I walked towards the woods, I passed little Jessie where she stood in her field.

"Hello, Jessie."

She didn't move.

I came closer. Through my darkness, I seen a glazed look in her eyes. "Well, I just wanted to say hi." Moving off, I looked back. She still hadn't moved. I knew how that felt now.

The firelight might have been dark, but inside the woods it was blacker than night. I felt around for a tree with space beneath it for me. Finding a good one, I slid my back down against the rough trunk till I hit the ground. Funny how it didn't scratch me none.

Closing my eyes, I waited for sleep to come, but it didn't. I looked up through branches I couldn't see to stars that might be hanging there and thought things out again. And again. By the middle of the night, I came to one conclusion.

There's got to be more to this. There just had to be, and I was gonna find it out. Yes sirree Bob, I would find it all out.

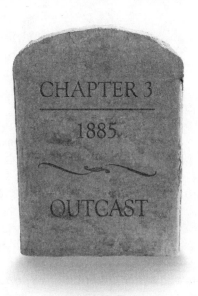

CHAPTER 3

1885

OUTCAST

Shadows are marked with darkness cause they're so dense with trouble.
—J. Johnson

I decided to meet this thing head-on. People knew more than they were telling. Horace for one. And Jessie. Them Shadows were more like me than anybody else. Why didn't they come back? And the noisy ones by the fire—loose-tongued as they were, I could find out a lot from them.

I left the forest for the dark night fire. They were there, all right, talking and laughing.

Passing little Jessie in the field, I stopped again. "Hi, Jessie."

Off in her own world, she didn't see me.

Laughter drew me to the fire. "Winston, you old fool," said a hag, "you never charmed a woman when you was alive. What makes you think you can get one now?"

"Some charmer," laughed an old guy. "Scares her half to death every time he calls on her."

Everyone howled.

The one this must have been about—Winston—turned to the old guy. Even through my darkness I seen the firelight pick up raised scars on the right side of his face. "I ain't done trying, Shamus. She ain't . . ." he mumbled a few words I couldn't hear, ". . . and I ain't giving up on her."

The group quieted.

"She feels it when I'm near. I know she does."

Nobody said nothing.

"Talks to me sometimes too."

"Oh, Winston," snorted the hag, "they all do that. Makes them feel better . . ."

I moved closer but missed some of what she said.

". . . might hear them, but they don't really believe it."

I entered the circle and they turned as one to look at me, then scooched in the other direction. Not to make room for me, no sir. To get away. They had looked so friendly, but now I seen no welcome here.

"Hello," I said anyway.

Silence first, then the hag—Eleanora—spoke. "Well, whaddya know."

"Didn't take long," said Winston.

The old guy looked me up and down. "Figured it'd be a while. Guess I was wrong."

I stepped back. "I . . . I don't know what you're talking about."

A big woman sitting on a log patted the spot next to her. "Honey, don't you listen to none of them. You come on over here to Mama."

"Oh, here she goes," said the old guy and they shrieked with laughter.

The big woman scowled. "Shamus, you done enough damage for one night."

"Dolores, you ain't *never* gonna give up!" he snapped back.

She leaned my way. "Don't pay him no mind, honey. You just come sit over here and everything will be all right."

I sat down a ways from her on the log. She inched towards me.

Shamus shook his head in disgust. "Ain't nobody too low for you, Dolores."

Something wasn't right—not just this woman making moves on me—something they seen in me.

One man stood. "I ain't watching this," he said and turned to leave.

Winston came to stand in front of Dolores. "Woman, what the HELL you think you doing? You know he ain't our kind."

What? Their skin looked the same as mine.

"I'll choose my companions, if you don't mind," said Dolores. "Hell's bells, ain't nobody our kind when you get down to it." She made a face and held her belly in pain.

Why was everybody hurting all the time?

"What you mean, I'm not your kind?" I asked.

"You different," said Winston. "We don't mix—your kind and us. It just don't work." He walked away and joined the others, who had moved off.

"All right." Dolores hefted herself up off the log. "You're right." She traipsed after the others into the night.

I up and followed. "Hey!" I yelled, but they weren't stopping. I jumped ahead and blocked them. They walked right through me! Just like Sammie when she fell near Mammy's shed. But Sammie was alive. From what Horace said, these folks were dead.

I jumped ahead again and walked beside Winston. "What do you mean I'm different?"

He wouldn't answer.

I jumped next to Shamus. "How are we different from each other?"

Finally, I jumped in front of Dolores and the group stopped as one.

Hands on her hips, she said, "Look. You don't know nothing 'bout nothing." She rolled her eyes to the sky as if asking for help then shook her head. "Everything's different for you now. You're just starting to understand. So here it is. You gots a shadow on you, and we don't."

They began to walk away.

"Wait!"

They stopped. Dolores turned. "What?"

"Just give me a minute. Please."

They laughed.

"What's so funny?"

Winston answered, "Cause there ain't no such thing."

"No such thing as what?"

"A minute!" said Shamus and they broke up again.

"This ain't funny!"

Dolores stepped forward and pointed. Her finger touched my chest. "You got to find things out for yourself."

Homer shook his head. "Don't know how you can get so close."

"Don't bother me none," she answered.

I held up my hands. "Explain one thing. Just one thing."

They waited.

"What you just said—that there ain't no minutes—how do you mean that?"

"Time . . . ," began Dolores. She shook her head. "I don't know how to say it. . . ."

Winston patted her shoulder. "Time ain't what you think it is."

"What do you mean?"

"It changes. Sometimes a minute ain't more than the snap of your finger. Other times, a minute is eternity."

They turned as one, leaving me midfield near Jessie.

I tried not to scare her. "Jessie."

She didn't answer.

I moved in front of her. "Jessie."

She blinked, focused, and looked at me.

"Jessie, what are you doing standing here all the time?"

She looked off again, but I stopped her. "Jessie, help me understand what you're doing. Please."

Her lips formed a word I could hardly hear. "Mama."

"What?"

Jessie gazed at the tent a ways from us.

"Your mother?"

A slight nod and she was off again.

"Jessie."

Her eyes came back.

"You're waiting for your mama?"

That slight nod and she started to go back.

"When you stand here and your thinking goes away, where does it go?"

She looked at me.

"What do you think about all the time you stand out here waiting for your mama?"

Her lips formed a circle. "Oh," she mouthed. "Life." At that, she was gone and I could see she wasn't coming back for a while.

So washed-out I could hardly stand, I stumbled to the fire pit, lay down, and conked out as the day dawned.

When I woke, it seemed like no time had passed, but it was night all over again. Folks talked while they cooked over the fire. Some sat near me or walked around me without thinking about it. Happened over and over. Nobody really sat in my spot, though it must have looked empty—the living folks, I'm talking about, not them dumb noisy night folk that came out after everyone went to bed. They were different. But for these folks who couldn't see me, it was like the space where I sat was taken and somehow they knew it.

I decided to experiment. Plenty came now to get their chitlins and looked for a place to sit. Most had their usual spots, but some moved around like I used to. Wondering what would happen if I sat in somebody's regular place, I sat in Mammy's. She came to stand in front of me, then talked and talked and talked to everybody.

"Mammy," said Joe next to me, "come rest your poor feet and sit down." He went to pat the spot where I sat, but suddenly his face screwed up.

"What's wrong?" asked Mammy.

"Don't know, just got a pain in my gut." He tried to smile. "You come sit by me and it'll be gone in no time."

But Mammy called, "Howard!"

An old soul with mangy hair going every which way, Howard's blue eyes saw right into you. Sometimes I wasn't so comfortable around Howard cause of it, but I knew him for a good person.

"Mammy, what you want, honey?" he asked.

"How come you don't come round my door no more?"

Everybody laughed as Mammy put her tin plate down on Joe's other side and waddled over to give Howard a hug.

She never did sit in her spot that evening. Nobody did.

Over the next few days, people avoided me no matter where I went. Suited me fine, since I wasn't feeling that warm towards them anyways. I used to be neighborly. I'd speak to people. Sort of. Well, not really, now that I thought about it and watched how much some talked and others didn't.

I was a barrel of laughs with a lady at my side, though. Life's tolerable when you gots yourself a good woman. Yes, sir. Made them laugh at night after having a good time rolling around. I'd raise my leg and we'd watch its silhouette move like nobody's should. Made them women scream—yes, I did— before, during, and after my time with them. Whether they were a-looking at my foot business or my other business, they loved being with Jeb Johnson.

I sat on a rock near the forest thinking about all this. By the time I got back to myself, everybody had left the fire except for passed-out drunks and Dolores and her gang. A burst of laughter as Winston danced up some foolishness.

I slumped against a tree stump. Except for Jessie and Old Horace, I had nobody to talk to. *Damn*. Rejected by my own kind. Again. I thought about all the lonely times I'd known in life, what with my gimpy foot and all.

I'd had my good times though too.

I smiled and remembered.

CHAPTER 4

1847

BEGINNING
BACKWARDS

The Path appears for you in a way that just couldn't be for no other.
—J. Johnson

I was born the son of slaves in a small shack before the
Civil War. Everywhere my mama went, I went too, cause I
couldn't walk like other babies. Papa made a small chair for me
that strapped on Mama's back. I'd sit backwards, looking
where she'd already been at what she no longer saw. I learned a
lot that way.

The other slaves stopped and talked with Mama. They
never paid me no mind cause I was always looking the other
way. But my mama, she talked to me cause I couldn't tell where
we were headed, just where we'd been.

"Here we go up the hill," she'd say, as my body leaned forward against the rung holding me in. I liked knowing what was
coming, even though I already guessed from the angle I hung at.

Massa Jim and Miz Emma let her take me up to the Big
House every day. There Mama worked and I would lie. Some

mornings it was so cold she wrapped me in as many blankets as she could get round me.

"Here we go to the well!" she'd say.

Strapped on her back, I watched the grass and trees sparkle with frost as we got water, first thing.

"Back to the wash shed."

Once we got there, she slipped me and my chair off her back in one piece. "Stay here while I put wood on the fire." Don't know why she said that. Wasn't like I was going nowhere.

I never did crawl like other babies and never walked till I was about five years of age cause my foot was almost on backwards. I remember standing on one leg when I was little, the other just not acting right when I leaned on it. I hobbled around, holding onto things, putting more and more weight on it, till the day came when I took my first step. That was a big day for me and my mama.

I stood in the middle of the dirt floor of the washing shed on one foot, not holding onto nothing. "Mama, look!"

Busy rubbing towels against the wash rack, she didn't hear me the first time.

"Mama, looky what I'm doing!"

She turned. Alone in the middle of the shed with nothing to hold me steady, I took a quick one-TWO.

She dropped everything. "Honey-child!"

So I did it again.

"Oh, my baby!" She ran over and swooped me into her arms, crying, "Oh, my darling boy! You gonna be all right now, ain't you?"

"Mama, let me do it some more."

She put me down. I settled in for a minute—my arms stretched out till I stopped swaying—took a big breath, stepped on my gimpy foot real quick, then back to my good one.

"Praise the Lord!" she cried.

I did it all over the little floor for her and started out the door.

"No!" she said, sweeping me off my feets. "Let them see you can walk and you're gone from me forever!"

I was so surprised, my eyes started to cry all by their selves. "But, Mama, they gonna be happy I can walk."

"They'll be happy all right. Put you to work in the fields soon as they see you're able, and that'll be the end of us." She looked right into my eyes. "Don't you *never* let them see you can walk, hear?"

I had felt so proud, and now we had to hide the biggest thing I ever done. In our shack though, she let me prance around and make everybody laugh. But we kept our secret, yes we did.

We had lots of secrets.

One night, our family sat at the supper table. We ate grits and cornbread, beans and cheese most the time. Wasn't bad the way Mama fixed it. We liked it plenty and came back for more when allowed. Our dog, a black and white mutt called "Hairy"—cause he was—always begged when we sat at the table. Hairy belonged to more than just our family. He ran around between all the shacks.

But Papa didn't like him. "I work hard all day just to feed you children," he used to scold. "I can't feed a dog too."

Still, Hairy looked so hungry—just skin and bones—I couldn't stand it no more. So I took some cornbread, making to put it in my mouth. When I slid my hand under the table, there it was.

Hairy wasn't dumb. He came over and got it.

"Mama!" yelled Sammy, my next biggest brother. "Jacobs just gived Hairy his dinner."

Hairy sat beside me, ears forward, and barked for more.

Mama came over and yanked me up by the ear. "Boy!" she yelled loud enough for everybody even at the Big House to hear. "You not hungry no more?"

You never talked back to Mama, so I hung my head and didn't say nothing.

"Well then, you can just go to bed."

I limped away from the table.

Next day, my brothers and sister teased me outside. "Gimpy got no dinner! Gimpy got no dinner," they sang, skipping around me in a circle. Other kids joined in. Pretty soon, the bunch hounded me cause I got no dinner and was skinny as a rat and couldn't skip and a whole lot of other reasons. I tried breaking through, but they closed in till I was down on the ground covering my head with my hands.

"That's e-*nough!*" Mama hollered from the front step. "You all get away now! Go on!" She must have bopped one of them good, cause they covered their heads to keep from getting hit again as they ran away.

When they were gone, she stood by me, alone. One hand held the broom, its bristles high, the other a fist on her hip. "Jacobs, what I gonna do with you? You're too old for me to keep saving you all the time. You got to find a way to keep safe by yourself."

I was too big for the chair now, so she picked me up by my elbows and hauled me to the Big House. I hid my eyes as she carried me through the back door and into the kitchen, ashamed that I still had to come to the house with her like a suckling. Plus, the tears from my crying just now might have shown.

Glory, the old cook, stirred something that smelled oh-so-good on the cooking stove. Turning as we came in, she gave me one look. "Hmph!" she snorted, and went back to stirring.

Mama set me on the milking stool in the corner, hung up her sweater, and put on a clean apron. "Just set here," she whispered. "We'll go to Miss Emily's room soon, hear?"

I nodded and looked around for Dusty, a real good mouser. I seen her get one or two flies, but she was better at mice. Every time old Doris or Glory screamed, "Mouse!" Dusty came running from out of nowhere. They'd get the broom and sweep that old mouse Dusty's way. That cat was fast. She was fat too.

Sometimes we worked together. If I seen one and pointed, she looked at my finger then ran for the mouse. Smart kitty. I knew she got it when I didn't see her for a while. Then she'd come out, licking her chops. We were a good team. Yes, we were.

Sometimes I played hide-and-seek with Dusty and sometimes with old Glory. The trick was to see how close I could get to Glory without her knowing. If she found me, she let me have it.

Mama hummed as she rushed in and out of the kitchen, getting laundry from the rest of the house—tablecloths, napkins, towels, rags, bed sheets, and the like. She wasn't no clothes laundress like Idy ("Tidy Idy," the kids called her). Mama did "linens." Idy and Mama worked together a lot but that don't mean they got along, cause they didn't. I was real good when Idy was around.

"Morning, Mabel." Miz Emma breezed into the kitchen on her morning visit and stuck her pretty white finger into Glory's chocolate batter.

"Morning, Miz Emma," answered Mama, bustling by with a load of sheets. This was Sheet Day then.

"Where's that fine boy of yours today?"

"Out in the fields with the rest of the children," Mama fibbed, kicking at me as she scurried by. I stuck my head back under the counter.

"Really? Is he that big now?"

"Oh, he not *that* big," covered Mama. "He just *thinks* he that big."

"Hmm," said Miz Emma. I could see her turn away from Mama. "I'd have thought he'd stay in the house, with his bad foot and all. Might be able to help with the linens."

"Well, now, that'd be a good idea, Miz Emma," said Mama, "but the boys want him in the fields."

It would be death for me with the other children if I was a laundry boy. Besides, I wanted to work in the fields, like them. No sir, I wasn't gonna be no woman's laundry boy. Not for nothing.

"I suppose if he's up to it, he ought to be in the fields," she said, turning to the day's menu.

Course, I wasn't in the fields. I was sitting by her right toe. Everybody knew it but Miz Emma.

Glory hummed a warning note as Miz Emma left the kitchen. "Mabel, you gonna get yourself in a heap of trouble," she said after the mistress left. "Let him be a laundry boy. Be good for him. Give him something to do 'sides crawling underfoot all day."

Mama scooped me up, an armload of sheets hiding me, and out we went to the laundry shack where Idy had the water already heated. Mama put me and the sheets down, lifted the kettle off the fire and poured hot water into the tub. Idy turned from Mama and straightened out a big dress she was fixing to iron. She and Mama never talked.

After a while, Mama came over to where I lay watching a bug crawl on the ceiling. She leaned over and I reached my hands up to her, ready for the fun part. Holding me under a stack of folded towels, Mama headed back to the Big House. We hurried through the vegetable garden, then the kitchen. I hid my face real good in Mama's bosom as we brushed through the swinging doors into the big dining room, the foyer, and up the stairs.

When we got to Miss Emily's room, she stooped over and I slid down through the towels and onto the rug. Going right for the closet, I reached for the knob. Mama turned it, put me inside, and shut the door.

CHAPTER 5

1852

HEAVEN

We're a whole lot more than we think.
—J. Johnson

The window at the end wall threw light into the closet. I crawled to the drawers under the shelves. After a lot of pulling, the bottom one moved out and a treasure trove slid open. Piles and piles of picture books lay waiting, my favorites on top. I lay down and disappeared into the pictures. By the time Mama poked her nose in again, I was lost in fairy tales and princes, pirates and jungles, soldiers and sailors.

It was heaven.

When Mama came back a long while later, she closed the door and sat down next to me. I crawled into her lap and she picked up our book, opened it to the spot where we left off yesterday, and began reading. I looked at the pictures, but sometimes she used a finger to keep her place as she read and I followed her finger, watching the words.

Back when they were little girls, Miz Emma and Mama played together. Miz Emma loved Mama and wouldn't let her go away, even during lessons, so Mama learned to read along-side Miz Emma. Mama's fingers ran across the letters now and I began saying the words with her. Her voice smiled, and it got to be a game. I got bigger and so did the words, till I didn't need her with me no more. And that's how come I learned to read.

One day she declared, "With that foot of yours, the only way you're gonna make something of yourself is if you can write too."

After that, we practiced letters in the closet. Nobody else knew.

Another day, she looked at the book I been reading and said, "You read books like this, you're gonna know all sorts of things others don't know 'less somebody tells them."

"Like Old Malcolm," I said, thinking of the old man in the Quarters. Everybody gathered round Old Malcolm at night when he told things he knew about the world cause he could read.

Back home, I loved my brothers—especially Henry, the old-est. He did things just to make me laugh, like crawling around on his hands and knees pretending to be Hairy. He even itched his ear with his foot—don't ask me how. Henry was so funny. Good too. Lots of times, he picked me up and took me outside, protecting me from the other kids when they made fun of me.

When I was old enough to get around without nobody's help, people didn't even recognize me.

"Who's that?" the men asked each other.

You'd think I came in out of the blue, they were so mixed up about who I was. I guess it was cause they were used to see-ing me always in somebody's arms or attached to someone's back, not out there all by myself. They never even seen my limp before, though Mama said everybody knew about my twisted foot when I was born. Sure had short memories.

"Why, that's Jacob's boy," said one. Least *he* knew who I was.

"Jacob's boy," they whispered to one another the first week I walked around outside all by myself.

"That's Jacob's," they said, nodding and pointing as I went by. And you know what? That's the name what stuck. I wasn't never known by nothing except who I belonged to. I didn't

even own my name, but I never thought about it. "Jacobs" is
what they called me, so that's what I went by. Maybe not having my own name made a difference in who I turned out to be.

One day, riding outside on Henry's back while he chased
the other children, I started to wriggle around.

"Let me down, Henry," I said.

"What?"

I squirmed, trying to get off. "Let me down. I wanna do it
myself."

"Jacobs, we're playing tag," said Henry. "You're always
gonna be 'It' if I let you down."

"I wanna try."

He put me down and I started to run after Taffy. Felt so
good, doing it myself.

The kids slowed up, then started to laugh. "Gimpy, gimpy,
gimpy," they teased.

"Dare you to call him that to my face!" Henry yelled, putting up his fists.

The little kids ran away, but the big ones poked around
with him a time or two. Then he let one have it and that was it.

He was my hero.

One day, Papa had to go off to hunt with Massa Jim. "He
needs help with the horses," Papa explained before he left.

"Why's it got to be you?" asked Mama, upset. He never left
home.

You could see in his eyes that Papa was plenty excited to go.
"I'll be back before you know."

A few days later, Massa Jim rapped at our door.

"Mabel? You in there?"

I got to the door first.

Hat in hand, he asked, "May I come in?"

The massa never came in our house before. Everybody outside gathered behind him to see why he did now.

Mama came and opened the door all the way for him.
"Where's Jacob?" she asked right off.

"Ma'am, I'm sorry to have to tell you this."

She clutched the dishrag to her bosom.

"There was an accident. A gun went off when it shouldn't
have and . . ."

She broke out howling like a dog. Bent over, she held her hands to her stomach and wouldn't stop. Neighbors stepped up on our porch. Seeing Massa Jim, they stayed out of the house, but they already knew. In the Quarters, word got around fast.

Everybody cried. Papa was gone, and Mama didn't have no way to take care of our place and work at the Big House too. We little ones would have to take care of it much as we could.

Lots of families here had no daddy. We just didn't think we would ever be one of them.

Now I got to tells you about the young massa—"Master" you'd call him, but we said "Massa" and I just can't get myself to call him nothing but that. His real name was James Jerome McIntosh III. His mama, Miz Emma, called him "James" or "Jamie."

One day, he tiptoed into the kitchen and snuck round a cupboard, laying low, waiting for Glory to move away from the pantry. He seen me hiding under the counter, winked, and—just like that—had me in his pocket. I stuffed down a giggle and kept a watch on old Glory for him. When the coast was clear, I gave him the high sign. He crept past me and slid into the pantry.

Glory seen the pantry door close, waddled over, and opened it to see what was what. "James Jerome McIntosh the Third! What you doing in my pantry?"

"Aw, come on, Glory," he said, his hands behind his back.

"You know your mama don't allow no sweets fore dinner. Let me see what you got in them hands."

"Aw, Glory."

"Show me."

Slowly, he brung his hands out and opened them to show two tiny chocolate cakes that you-all would call "cookies."

Glory took them from his grimy hands. "Git on over to that wash basin and clean up."

Massa's eyes followed the cookies on their way to the garbage bin. "If I wash, can I have one?"

She stood there, hands on hips, while he marched over and washed up with lye soap. Drying his hands on an old rag, he turned around to ask for one now that his hands were clean, but Glory done moved on.

"Someday, when I'm big and have my own plantation, will you be my head cook, Glory?" he asked, smoothing her over.

"That day be a long way off, Massa Jamie. Today, I gots to take care of what we gonna eat—and NOT eat," she steamed. "Now run along out of the kitchen."

He turned to go.

"And don't be snooping round here no more," she called after him.

He passed through the swinging doors into the dining room, the top of a cookie peeking from his back pants pocket.

Everybody loved young Massa Jamie, especially me. A soft-skinned boy with curly blond hair, rosy cheeks, and bright blue eyes, he had a laugh that made everybody smile and a way that charmed. He was everything I wasn't and did everything I couldn't. Lots of times, he'd look up and see me in the window or catch my eye from one of my hiding places and give me a wink. I'd back away so nobody else would catch me. We were about the same size—maybe even the same age.

One day, I was in the closet a-looking at a picture book, then looking out the window, dreaming about life and the goings-on at the plantation. I wondered what it would be like to be young Massa Jamie, riding his pony with his daddy, learning to shoot and hunt, playing trains in his room. How I wished to play with those trains, but Mama never let me. Might get too interested in what-all he had there and get into mischief. I think the only reason she let me be in Miss Emily's room is cause I had no liking for girl things—just the books. Plus, Miss Emily went away to school. I wouldn't get into trouble there.

Every so often, young Massa Jamie came into Miss Emily's room, though he wasn't supposed to. I'd watched through a crack in the closet door when he snuck in, hoping he wouldn't come in and upset the applecart.

Course, it had to happen. The closet door opened. Midst turning a page, I froze. Massa came in, looked under Missy's hanging clothes, and rummaged through the toy boxes. He kept moving my way—it was a long closet—looking for something, till he nearly knocked into me. We both cried out from fright when he saw me—dark and still as a statue, my eyes big and wide.

His fright turned to anger. "What are you doing here?"

I didn't say nothing.

He stood up and got hold of hisself—remembering he wasn't supposed to be there neither—and whispered, "I said, what are you doing here, boy?"

I couldn't move and didn't say nothing.

Massa glanced at the closet door. "Look," he whispered near my ear, like we was in on it together. "You don't tell anyone I've been here, and I won't either. Deal?"

He held out his hand.

Scared, I whispered, "All right," then did something I ain't never done before or since. I shook the hand of a white person. Our hands were nearly the same size. Oh, his fingernails were clean and mine dark and dirty, but otherwise our hands looked about the same. Now, I done looked at people's hands all my life. You can tell a lot by someone's hands. He didn't have no cuts on his like I did. But he bit his nails and, sure as shooting, so did I.

I looked up into his eyes while we shook hands and saw something I didn't expect: fear. This boy was afraid I'd turn him in and get him in trouble. I never thought a white man could be afraid of a colored, but there it was in his eyes. I've seen that look on a white man's face since, and it ain't pretty, cause he don't trust coloreds—thinks we gonna hurt him one way or another. But I wouldn't do that.

I think he seen I was just as afraid, cause all of a sudden his eyes softened and got real nice. He didn't make hisself real proud or nothing like he could have. In fact, he smiled a right friendly smile. I relaxed and maybe even smiled back a little.

"What's your name?" he asked.

"Jacobs."

He sat down next to me and looked at my book, then at my legs and bare feets. "What's the matter with your foot?"

"Don't know. It just don't work right," I said. "Always been like that."

He looked at the book I'd been reading—well, looking at, as I was real young yet. My mouth hung open as I watched him watching me.

"You like books?" he asked.

I nodded.

"I like books too." He reached for the book and I let him have it, slipping my hands under my thighs as I sat next to him. "This is a good one," he said. "You come here often?"

I nodded again.

"To do this?" He pointed at the book.

Another nod.

He looked at the book. "This one's about trains." He leafed through the pages. "You like trains?"

I nodded harder.

"I got a train set in my room. You seen it?"

Getting into dangerous territory, I shook my head just a little.

"You wanna play with it?"

I nodded real hard.

Forgetting what he came for, he crept to the closet door, opened it a crack and looked out. "C'mon," he whispered, waving for me to follow.

I stayed where I was.

"Don't you wanna come?" he asked, then looked about the room. "Nobody's gonna see us. They're all out today. Only old Buster's here." Buster the Butler, the old houseman, was hard of hearing. Good thing, too.

Massa Jamie went to the doorway, peeked into the hall, then came back. He looked at me troubled-like, glancing at my foot. "You can't walk," he said.

"Not real good." Fact was my thump-THUMP walk would wake the dead.

"Can you stand?"

I stood up.

He turned around and scooched down. "C'mon," he said over his shoulder.

I knew what he wanted from Henry doing the same thing.

"Hop on."

I did. Both of us schooled in the art of spying, we looked out the door, my head 'top his. The coast was clear and out we went. Massa closed the door, peeked around the corner, and we hurried down the hall, then crossed into his room—something I never in a million years thought I'd do.

He put me down and said, "Wait here." Sticking his head into the hallway for one last look-see, he popped back in and shut his door. He reached under his bed. "Look at this!" He slid out a big board nearly the length of the bed and just as wide. On it lay tracks and a locomotive with five cars and a caboose.

I couldn't say nothing.

Massa Jamie showed me how to push the train on the tracks. I got on my knees and moved it around. He made chugging sounds, whistling like real trains do. Then he went to a cupboard and got out a bunch of little wooden soldiers and horses and rode them up to attack the train.

It was the best day of my life, till Mama came looking. She got so riled up, I wasn't allowed to go back to the Big House for the rest of the week. My sister had to take care of me, but that was all right. Nothing could wipe the smile off my face.

Now I had two real heroes to help me in my two worlds: my brother Henry, who protected me outside the Big House, and my new friend inside. Safer and more loved than ever before, I thought myself set for life. This would never change.

CHAPTER 6

1860

CHANGES

Most everybody's got their own Civil War going on inside theirselves.
—J. Johnson

"Where's that fine-looking oldest boy of yours, Mabel?"

The boss-man overseer stood at our door with nobody behind him. Everyone ran with their tails between their legs whenever he came round.

Not Mama. If nothing else, she was just the opposite. Mama knew what he was about. That day, she knew what he wanted. It might be a losing battle, but Mama was not gonna let that man have it without a fight.

Shooing us behind her with her dishrag, she stuck her chest out farther than usual and said, "Who wants to know?" like she didn't know.

"I hear he's ready for the fields."

They put children in the fields here practically soon as they could walk, which meant I wouldn't be going for a really long time.

"Says who?"

"How old would he be now, Mabel?"

"We don't count birthdays like you white folk."

"Missy, I know a strong boy when I see one. Now, I seen your boy the other day and he's right ready for the fields. Get him on out here."

"My oldest ain't here. But I don't think you mean mine. He's just a small boy."

Without asking, the man opened the door. "I better see about that." He walked in, white as white and tall as the ceiling.

All us children shrunk back, trying to disappear into the walls. I crawled behind the rest and looked out between them.

"Well, now, look at this," said the boss-man. "Nice bunch of young'uns you got, Mabel."

Something real bad was gonna happen.

"Don't know 'em. They ain't mine," Mama said.

I started to cry, but the others pushed at me to shut up. Funny how a person can control hisself when he has to.

"They're yours," he said, pulling Henry out by the arm and eyeing the rest of us. "But this one's mine."

At that, we all cried.

"That's my baby," screamed Mama.

But it was useless. That white man hoisted a screaming Henry over his shoulder and out the door just like that.

Field hands slept in larger shacks—men and women separated—unless they had children. Then they slept with their young families. We'd see Henry around and at prayer meeting and big celebrations, but it wouldn't never be the same as having him home with us.

Following year, the boss-man came to get my sister, and he didn't take her to no field, neither. No, sir. That boss-man fetched her all the way to Selma to sell her to the highest bidder. She was pretty but dumb—never no good at house chores—so I didn't understand what value she could bring.

I never seen her again.

Next in line was you-know-who, but Mama wouldn't let them see me at my best. She'd catch and paddle me when she caught me showing off.

"They see you moving around like that, only a matter of time till you'll be gone too," she warned.

They didn't come get me for the fields or for soldiering for a long time. But as I think about it now, I do believe it had more to do with Massa Jamie needing a friend than it did with my bum foot. Back then, Massa Jamie had honor. He knew what I could and couldn't do and, true to his word, kept it secret. Together we grew from trains and soldiers to slingshots, bows and arrows, and finally, guns.

Mama wasn't sure what to think. "That boy's just like Miz Emma when she was little," she said one night as she fixed dinner. "Nobody else to play with—no brothers, no pets. When Miss Emily's here, she don't have nothing to do with him. His daddy's too busy to give him the time of day. Other children don't come to play either." Shaking her head, she stirred the gravy around in a pan. "It just ain't right."

I sat down at the table. "He has me," I said. "I'm glad he don't have nobody else."

She stopped stirring and nodded. "Long as you two get along, nobody makes you work the fields." She started stirring again. "That's one good thing. By the time they do . . ."

By the time they did, my voice would be changing and hair sprouting all over my body. It seemed a long way off.

Me and young Massa were always together. We spied on everybody and everything. Extra good at shinnying up trees, I could stretch way out on the branches. Tried to spy on Miss Emily that way when she was home, but she caught us every time.

One time, though, we had ourselves a ball watching the ladies in the parlor readying for a nap after a big picnic lunch. They stayed the entire day, and don't you know they all went in and shut the door, but not the curtains, and shed their fancy dresses right down to their bloomers! Our eyes full, we learned a lot that day.

Most of us slaves liked our life, such as it was. Massa Jim and Miz Emma were good, kind people. Course, the boss-man overseer was a different story. Plus, breaking up families like they did wasn't right, but none of us on that plantation knew any better. Fact is, we got reports from other plantations on how things could be a whole lot worse.

"We're the lucky ones," Mama would say, putting a nice face on it. "We got roofs over our heads and food in our stomachs," she declared. "More than some."

Some day I would learn that putting a nice face on bad things can get you in a heap of trouble. Understand, this all happened in the last days of slavery. Some owners were out to prove who was boss. You'd think, knowing they might someday lose their slaves, they'd be extra nice to us. But they weren't.

We got into plenty of our own fights too. That never changed before or after the War. It just didn't feel right between our own people no more. Slavery and loyalty got mixed up for some, especially the house servants. Old Buster the Butler and his wife went everywhere with Massa Jim and Miz Emma and defended them every time.

One afternoon, a group of neighboring plantation owners came riding up unexpected to speak with Massa Jim, taking everybody by surprise. Later, the house help came down to tell us about it at the campfire. Mama held me close as we gathered round to hear the news. Even though I really didn't have no idea what all was going on, the words from that night still ring in my ears.

Jesse, a young field worker, asked, "What upset those owners today?" Jesse done proved hisself a man to men and women alike. Everybody listened when he talked.

Old Daniel from the servants' quarters at the house spoke up. "I brung refreshment and cigars to the library." His gray beard glittered in the firelight along with his eyes. "Massa had me close them double doors, but I still heared real good."

Faces grew bright as everybody leaned in to listen.

"Massa Jim asked what they planned to do about it," Daniel said.

"Do about what?" asked Jesse.

Matthew, a boy about Henry's age, spoke up. "Why, the insurrection, that's what!"

People called Matthew "that young upstart." Henry sat next to him, his eyes alight. Mama didn't like Henry hanging around Matthew.

"Mighty big word, 'insurrection,'" somebody in back grumbled.

"Insurrection, hmph!" declared Bartholomew, the stable master. "You mean, stirring up trouble." He heard things while he helped the ladies and gents out in the barn who talked like he wasn't there.

"It's gonna be trouble if they *don't* stir something up," said Matthew.

"Massa Jim had something to say about that," said Daniel. "He says Alabama needs to get along with the rest of the states so they can keep trading with each other."

"Get along with which states?" asked Jethro. "North or South?"

Old Daniel shook his head. "Don't matter. The others talked about getting their government people to pull out."

"Pull out of what?" asked Matthew.

"The state government," said Daniel.

"What!" exclaimed someone in back. "We wouldn't be the state of Alabama no more?"

"That's how they're talking."

"Now, why they gonna do a fool thing like that?" asked another. "We ain't got no soldiers. Who's gonna defend us?"

"They talked about setting up their own government to keep their slaves," said Daniel. "Otherwise, the U.S. of A. might not let them."

That set everyone off. "Nobody tells Alabama they can't have slaves!" said Bartholomew, who liked the idea of being cared for, even if the price was his own freedom.

"Massa Jim ain't for it," said Daniel. "Neither am I."

Some wouldn't speak up in front of the house servants who liked Massa Jim's ideas of keeping things like they were. But later, low voices behind our shanty carried in through the little window above my bed. I heard them clear as a bell.

"Them house folks too cozy with the massa and missus." I made out the voice of Johnny-Boy, a young field hand. "House folk don't think about the good of their own people."

"Got that right," said a voice I couldn't place. "They's so happy they's 'cared for' by their owners," he mimicked in a singsong voice. "You call this cared for?"

All my life, I heard grumbling about one thing or another. It's easy to get hepped up against somebody else. Fact is, every generation has wars on the outside. If not against another country, it's another party, another religion, another people. Closer yet—make it against a friend, relative, or spouse. Just make it somebody else till you ain't got nobody to fight but yourself. Then you gonna see what the fighting's all about. Took me a while to get to that point, but I would. Oh, yes, I would.

Massa Jamie and me became blood brothers in a ceremony like the Injuns did. Taking a dagger, he slashed his forearm just enough to draw blood, then I slashed mine. We pressed our cuts together and exchanged blood. Holding a rag to his wound, Jamie held up his Bible.

"Put your left hand on the Bible and your right hand in the air," he commanded.

My left hand on the Bible, I lifted my right hand high over my head.

"No, stupid," he said, pulling my arm down. "Like this." Dropping the Bible, he used both hands to hold my arm out from my shoulder, bend my elbow and raise my hand.

"Now." He picked the Bible back up.

I put my left hand on it.

Looking me in the eye, he said, "Repeat after me: I swear, by all the saints in the Bible . . ."

I repeated just like he said.

". . . that you, Massa Jamie, are my blood brother and that I, Jacobs, am yours. I will always come to your aid, wherever and whenever you call, from this time forward."

I said it for him, then he swore it for me. We meant it heart and soul—at the time.

Our way of life didn't really change till the men started leaving to be soldiers—first the whites and their colored servants, then anybody who could carry a gun. Never thought that would be me, but you never know what life's gonna bring. When Alabama seceded from the Union, war finally broke out. Massa Jim up and left, taking some of the servants for him and his horse. Buster the Butler was too old to go, but he did take Jesse and Matthew.

"Thank God he didn't take Henry," praised Mama.

Massa Jamie wanted to go, but his pappy said he was too young. Did young Massa put up a fuss!

"Wants to go to war and prove he's a man. But men get killed," Mama said. "All that proves is he's mortal like everyone else."

When I wasn't reading or playing with Massa Jamie, Mama made me help iron and fold up at the house. I didn't know why Mama still hid me.

"Ain't like I look able-bodied, doing women's work," I grumbled.

I loved the books in that house though. Way past the ones in the closet now, Massa Jamie got me big books from the house library to take home. I stole away with his daddy's books, careful to keep them nice, trading them in for more when I was done. Thirsty for knowledge, I listened to white folk and learned to talk like them. Had a knack for talking like whoever I was around. Back in the slave quarters, wanting to be one of *them*, I laid all that aside and spoke just like always. Still do, though every now and again you notice some word that don't fit. That'd be me to a tee. I never quite fit anywhere I went.

His father gone, Massa Jamie was out to prove who was boss now, even when we played together. He'd look at me and say, "Jacobs, get me that," and I'd say, "Yes, Massa," like a good boy.

Ordering me around when I couldn't do it back changed our friendship. We weren't the same after all.

At night in the Quarters, we could hear him argue with Miz Emma all the way up at the Big House.

"Shut up!" he yelled. "I'm sick of you crying all the time!"

Sitting at the fire, we quieted, not so we could hear—no, that ain't the reason. We all got quiet cause it made us sad for Miz Emma.

"I said I don't want to hear it!" he yelled.

Most of us thought the world of that lady.

"Bullshit!"

We'd shake our heads and go inside ourselves.

"Let me leave, then!"

A cry, then something in the house shattered.

Somebody by the fire hummed a tune. Others joined in to drown out the noise. We had enough trouble. Didn't need to hear it up there too. Soon everybody sang a song about crossing the river and going home. Didn't take long for them to go back to their shacks. The few that were left stared into the fire, alone in thought.

After a while, Massa Jamie and I didn't play together no more. Instead, I spent my extra time at home. Too much time on anyone's hands ain't good. For a boy about to be a man, boredom is the devil's playground. I started getting into fights—scuffles at first, then out-and-out brawls. Frustrated with the loss of my friend, I fought to show everybody, including me, that I wasn't no sissy.

Out of nowhere they'd appear, swarming around me as I walked back from the Big House. "Gimpy's doing girls' work," Marcus Gregory said one day.

"Yeah," said Lester the Fester as they followed me up our steps. "And he reads so many books, he could be a schoolmarm!"

"Schoolmarm! Schoolmarm! Gimpy is a schoolmarm!" they chorused. Others joined in, wolves ready for the kill.

"Without your bestest friend no more, you ain't nothing," shouted another.

"Never was," said Marcus Gregory.

Till then, I never knew how they felt about my friendship with Massa Jamie. Without his protection and with Mama still up at the house, they seen their chance to get back at me and jumped on it. I got to our shack all bloodied up and stayed in bed the rest of the day.

Another morning, I stopped at the well before going up to the Big House.

"Why, ha-llo, Miz Gimpy," said Marcus Gregory, pulling up water for his family. "How's the Laundry Lady today?" He thought he was tough stuff cause he had two names.

"That boy ought to watch his mouth," Mama said a long time ago when he started picking on me. "Truth is, he don't know why he has two names instead of one, like normal people."

"Do you know why he does?" I asked.

She looked at me, then made a decision. "I'm gonna tell you something. And don't you never tell nobody else. Hear?"

I nodded.

"Truth about that boy's fancy two names is this: His mama didn't know which to choose. Know why she couldn't decide?"

I shook my head.

"Cause she didn't know which proud papa to name him after."

I didn't get it.

"You know Old Marcus."

"Yes," I said.

"And you know Old Gregory?"

Ohhhh . . .

"Each was so proud to be that boy's papa, she didn't want to disappoint neither, so she named him after both. Now, how do you like that?"

And here I didn't even have a name to call my own.

"Turned them two men into laughingstocks, and rightfully so—strutting around like peacocks," she muttered.

I thought about names. To this day, I still don't know my real one. Never did ask Mama. Don't know why, I just didn't. I was too young when he died to ever really get to know the man I was named after. My name probably made about as much sense to me as Marcus Gregory's did to him.

Marcus Gregory had names for me, though, and let me hear them whenever he could.

Came to a point where I had to prove myself, but my timing was all off. "What'd you call me?" I asked at the well hole that morning. Sticking my chest out, I limped over and shoved my chin in his face.

Littler than me when I stood up straight, he sure had a chip on his shoulder. So did I, I guess.

We drew a right good crowd and, hearing the ruckus, somebody big pulled me off Marcus Gregory and held me from behind. I seen the color of his arms and twisted to see who it was, but his voice said it all.

"Whoa, now, what's going on here?"

Everyone hushed.

Marcus Gregory backed off.

The struggle over, Boss-man let me go, stepped back and looked us over. We always tried to stay out of his way. He was searching for replacements cause so many already went off to war. We should have known he'd be lurking around the Quarters fore everyone went off to their jobs.

"You two ought to be working in the fields instead of wasting all this energy on a fight," he said.

The big question everybody wanted to ask was why Boss-man wasn't going off to war hisself?

He yanked us by the collar and hauled us away as the women screamed.

"We're gonna put that energy to good use!"

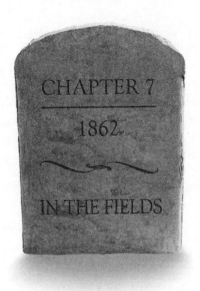

CHAPTER 7

1862

～

IN THE FIELDS

There's things you can change and things you can't.
—J. Johnson

Marcus Gregory blamed me. "Stay away from Jacobs!" he warned as we worked the cotton rows. "He'll get you in trouble." Everybody knew what happened, but he wouldn't let it alone. Taunted me all day in the fields. And he wasn't the only one.

Now I understood why Mama wouldn't let me out of her sight when I used to want to be her errand boy.

"Mama, please let me go by myself," I used to say when we went out to get something.

She leaned over me, her finger in my face. "Listen to me," she began. "I don't know where you get to thinking it's a kind world out there." She straightened, sighed, and looked away. "Ain't your fault you was born this way." Then she looked straight at me. "I ain't always gonna be around to protect you, but while I can, I'll be right by you."

I didn't know what she meant, excepting I'd be tied to her, ball and chain, till I got big.

Sometime later, she talked with Henry while they cut flowers under the window above my bed.

"Jacobs's foot's like that for a reason," she said.

"What you talking about, Mama?" Henry asked.

I wanted to know too, so I stood and pressed myself against the wall to hear better.

"Don't never tell nobody what I'm 'bout to say, Henry."

"All right, Mama."

"You promise?"

"I said all right, didn't I?" Henry hardly ever got mad. He calmed his voice. "What is it?"

"Remember how things was between your daddy and me when I was carrying your little brother inside me?"

Henry didn't say nothing. Maybe he nodded, maybe not.

"Remember how we was always at each other's throats?"

"Mama! You and Daddy never choked each other."

"No, no. That's not what I mean." She stopped. "I ain't saying this right."

"Tell me what you mean."

"Back then, your daddy and I argued a lot."

"I remember that, all right."

"Okay then," she said. "I went around with my head in a dark cloud all day every day, mad about every little thing. And look what happened."

Henry was quiet a minute. "What?"

Now Mama lost *her* temper. "What happened?" She sounded like she couldn't believe her ears, like what she just said should have made sense to the dumb old chickens and piglets running around the Quarters. "What happened is the boy got twisted up inside me cause I was twisted up inside."

I slid down onto the mattress.

"Aw, Mama," said Henry, "that's not why it happened."

"You got a better reason?"

"I don't know. Maybe his foot got twisted cause it was in the wrong danged place. Wasn't no room for it to turn right at the beginning, so it just growed that way. Like plants up against a wall take the shape of whatever they lean against."

I liked Henry's reason better.

Next morning as Mama and I walked to the Big House, I had something on my mind. "Mama?"

"Yes, sugar?"

"What's a omen?"

"An omen?" She looked down at me as we climbed the hill. "Why you asking 'bout omens?"

Nobody believed like Henry did about my foot. Old women looked me in the eye and made the hex sign if I came near at certain times, like before a storm. Laughter and talking stopped whenever I came to the sitting fire after I was big enough to be without Mama. And ladies-with-child stayed out of my path.

"Oh," I said, trying to make it seem like it wasn't important, "Helene and some of the others said I was a bad omen when I came on them sudden-like and surprised them."

Mama frowned and slowed down. "Oh, they did, did they?" On came her Protecting Face. "What else did they say?"

I looked at the birds flying, the pretty flowers growing up by the house, the blue sky. "Oh, nothing."

But she stood there till I let it all out.

"They just screamed and ran away." I started walking again. "That's all."

One day, I read in a book about an "outcast." The instant I seen that word, I knew that was me—an outcast. Here I was out in the fields working alongside the others like I always dreamed! First day, I worked alone—ignoring Marcus Gregory, listening to them sing, trying to join in and be part of it all. But it wasn't to be. No sirree. One minute everybody's singing but me. Then I'm singing all by my lonesome. Same thing with the joking and bantering back and forth.

"Hey, Leroy, you old coot," Jessie Lee yelled at the old man picking cotton in the next row.

"What you want, Jessie Lee?"

Everybody knew Leroy had a hankering for Jessie Lee. She wouldn't have none of it, but she liked to tease.

"You coming by later?"

The rest hooted it up, saying Leroy was too old to make any female happy.

"What you want me to come by for?" he asked.

"She wants you to rub her back," yelled somebody.

"She wants some of your sweet corn pone," answered someone else.

"What she don't want you can't give her no-how."

Everybody laughed.

I looked around with a smile, glad to be there. Soon as I started laughing though, they went back to work.

"What you laughing at?" asked Jessie Lee.

"You don't even know what they's talking about," said another.

All my hopes and dreams turned to dust as I chopped weeds out of that dry soil.

Funny thing about getting what you pray for. You think, *If I could do that or be that, I'd be free and happy as a lark.* But it ain't never what you thought and just brings a whole new set of problems. Was that way when I learned to walk and couldn't show nobody, and now it was that way working as a field hand. I had prayed for both with my whole heart, and both brought problems I never could have guessed. And this wasn't nothing compared to other dreams that would come true down the road.

But a man can't stop dreaming. Without dreams, he ain't got a leg to stand on, even if he does have two good feets.

Didn't take long to learn how to work them fields. I picked so fast, my hands got to be a blur. In fact, I worked them too good.

"Jacobs, who do you think you are?" Fat Fannie asked from her row as I sped by.

I didn't say nothing, just kept working like I was supposed to.

At lunch, Old Jeremy took me aside. "What you trying to prove, son?"

I looked at him, troubled.

"You can't keep up a pace like that. Gonna wear yourself out. Besides, you make the rest of us look bad."

"I don't want to make nobody look bad," I said. "Just aiming to do my best."

Fat Fannie pricked up her ears, came over, and spoke at me from behind, making me jump. "From now on," she said, "why don't you just move along like the rest of us?"

That's the last time I ever tried to let someone notice the good work I did.

Things were different at home too. Why they let me stay with Mama now that I was in the fields, I don't know. But it didn't bother me like I thought it would. So now it was me and Mama and my younger twin brothers that always got into it. I couldn't stand their fights. Maybe it bothered me cause of all the fights I got into now. It didn't matter where I went, anyone called me a name or even snickered at my foot, I let them have it. I was a man. Respect me or pay.

Then there was Massa Jamie. Now that he was in charge, I'd see him strut around the plantation. Never even nodded when we passed. Made me sad. Even more, it made me mad. My best friend not too long ago, now he didn't want nothing to do with me. Looked on the outside like he thought hisself better than me, but I knew that—deep down inside—we were the same.

I worked without recognition from no one, not even Mama. She was so busy up at the house. They done took the old butler and all the housemen to be servants for officers in Massa Jim's regiment. When she came home each day, she had no time to do more than throw food together for the rest of us.

Tired from working in the fields, I couldn't worry about Massa Jamie. Our friendship was doomed from the beginning anyway. Look at Mama and Miz Emma. So close when they were little, now they were mistress and laundress and that was that. Made me wonder if Mama felt like I did.

"Mama," I asked as she fried up some onions.

"Hmmm?"

"Mama, I was wondering."

She kept stirring. "What?"

"You know how you and Miz Emma was good friends when you were little?"

"Yes."

The pan sizzled as she added chicken pieces.

"When you stopped being friends, how did you feel?"

She looked at me and I looked down, my feelings too plain.

"I knew for a long time it was coming, cause I knew my place." She began stirring again. "Why?"

"Just wondering."

She kept cooking, adding greens now.

My mouth started to water. Sure looked good.

"You seen the way Massa Jamie swaggers around the place, now his daddy's gone? You want to be best friends with somebody like that?"

He'd changed for the worse. That's why we couldn't be friends no more.

"Thank you, Mama. You're right."

"Don't you worry none. You gonna have plenty of friends before your day is through. See if it ain't so when your time comes."

I brightened, but she darkened.

"Just watch that you don't end all those friendships with fights. You ain't no better than nobody else and you ain't no worse. Remember that second part or you'll try all your life to show people who's best. You just need to satisfy one person—you."

"Mama, I don't know how to be like I'm just as good as everybody else. Look how I walk."

"Look at old Nelson. You think he's less of a man cause he can't see?"

"No, ma'am."

"And what about Baby Lee?" Three years old and couldn't say a word, but she was cute as a button. "Think she's less of a child cause she can't talk?"

"You're right, Mama. She's just as good as the next baby. Maybe more, cause of her cute little ways. But I don't have no cute ways. I'm dumb and ugly and no good to nobody."

That did it. She slid the skillet off the fire. "How many times I gotta tell you? God don't make no man on this green earth that don't have something good about him. Go lie down and don't come back till you think of five good things about yourself."

Dinner was coming and me starving, so I thought fast. Later, sitting at supper, I believe my eyes shone more than the candles as I looked around, grateful for each one in my life—even my pesky twin brothers.

Massa Jamie was full of hisself, partly due to the way his Mama doted on him. I remembered how, when I was little and hiding in the house, she prattled on in the kitchen about "Massa Jamie this" or "Massa Jamie that!"

That made Massa Jamie mighty big in my eyes then. So when the day came for us to be friends—well, that was about the biggest good thing that could ever happen to me. Which is why losing him was the worst.

But Massa Jamie wasn't like he used to be, and I decided I didn't want him for a friend no more. Much. Sure had been fun though—fooling around in that house, getting to have the same privileges he did. I didn't even mind being his "boy" when that time came. Not really. In a way, I wanted to be his boy. Made me special.

One thing that hadn't changed was the way his mama doted on him. She used to come in just to watch us play. "You're so smart, Jamie! I declare, you can do anything." She'd ruffle his hair before leaving the room.

"I wish she'd cut that out," he'd say, disgusted.

But he must have liked it some and took it to heart, cause he started acting more and more like he expected her to hand everything to him. After a while though, his mother's doting turned him from her. All the girls working up at the house talked about their arguments.

"Stop it!" he yelled now.

"But, Jamie, honey. You're just a child."

"I am not! I'm old enough!" he said and ran out of the room.

Happy when the boss-man overseer had to go to the battlefields, we didn't count on things turning worse. Frustrated young Massa Jamie was the only one left who could work us. I'd worked the fields for a good year by then. The second time I got in a fight after Massa Jamie took over, he ran me off the field.

"You get home, boy." He yelled like he never even knew me. "I'll make sure you *never* come back."

I got to our shack and lay down on my pallet. Mama was still at the Big House. Luther and Cornelius beat her home. They ran in yelling and raising a ruckus but stopped when they seen me.

"What you doing home?" asked Luther.

"None of your business."

"You in trouble again?"

I turned to the wall.

"You *are* in trouble, ain't you?"

I pulled the blanket over my face.

They ran outside, yelling the news, but something hushed them up real quick. I heard a scuffle, then footfalls on the steps. The screen door opened and closed. Somebody big was in the house.

"Get your things." It was Massa Jamie. "Now. You're going away."

I rolled over. "What about Mama? She can't . . ."

"Your mama's crying up at the Big House after hearing what you did today. Now get your things or not, because you're leaving." He stomped out and waited on the step.

This man had been my best friend. Now he was my worst enemy.

In shock, I looked around at the little place I called home. I'd miss the nice feeling my mama made here. I looked at the pots and pans hanging above the stove, at the cloth pieces she had worked on just last night to make a new blanket for one of us.

I was gonna miss my mama. I surely would.

Outside, I heard crying and a crowd coming closer.

Oh no. It was happening all over again, just like when they sold my sister and my older brothers. Only this time it was for me.

Oh Lord, I'll never see her again.

The noise grew till a bunch of them came up the stairs. Massa Jamie went down the way to wait. The door opened, and there they were—a bunch of sad folks all looking at me. Mama stood in the middle, tears streaking her face, her head kerchief falling to the side. She cried out, lost her balance, and looked up at the ceiling as she fell back against the others.

"Here now, Missy," said old Joe. "Here now. Stand up and be strong for your boy. He gots to see he comes from strong people—you and all the rest of us—so he can be strong now. Hear? Stand up now."

And Mama, she did stand and so did I. We stood there, both of us so scared we didn't know what to say. She sniffed and her eyes started to fill and then she was all over me—her tears wetting my shirt, my tears wetting her blouse.

What would I do without her to help me through? How could I live without knowing she would hold me up, even though I could walk now?

She held my head to her, and we cried and cried, swaying back and forth. "My baby, my baby, my baby," she wailed.

Others moaned cause what was coming for them wasn't much different.

Oh Lordy, Lordy, Lordy, I thought. I wished I'd kept my temper in them fields. I wished I hadn't been so mad. I wished I didn't have to show everybody I was a man. I wished I never had that foot, that bad old foot that twisted my insides till they was just like my outsides—and twisted up my life even more.

Damn that foot. Damn me for being born with it. Damn me for just plain being born, I thought.

Somebody brung up a cart pulled by an old mule and put me in back. Everybody stood around to say goodbye.

I watched them all gathered together, all of us damp in tears, and could only think one thing—*What's happening to us?*

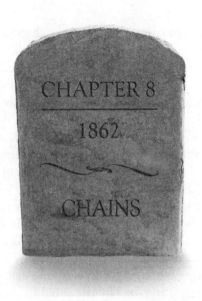

CHAPTER 8

1862

CHAINS

What is, is.
—J. Johnson

At first, I looked back at everybody, then at the plantation, then at the fields we passed, saying goodbye in my head to everything and everybody I'd ever known. Oh, I deserved it for getting into fights all the time and then—well—for being gimpy.

Then I got to wondering, *Who would buy a gimp?*

Massa Jamie had put manacles on my feets but not my hands, so I could move around easy but wouldn't run away. Silly. I couldn't run if I wanted to. I didn't even think of running away—at least not then.

Having never set foot off the plantation, that ride to the sale opened my eyes. As we trekked along in the cart, houses and shacks took my eye—some right fine houses too. Hands in the fields stopped to watch us go by. Must have been pretty obvious where I was headed with manacles on my feet and all.

In some fields, it looked like whole families worked together side by side: mother, father, sister, brother, grandpappy—all of

them. You could tell cause they all wore the same color head-
scarf. And over here another family wore a different-colored
kerchief. Least that's what I figured. Never heard of nothing
like that before. Where we were, girls and boys and men
worked the fields. Mostly, the women tended the Big House.

After a while, I fell asleep. Must have been real tired, cause
when I woke up, it was night and noisy as hell. Torches lit the
place along the way. Surrounded by carts, creaking wagons, and
jangling horses—their drivers yelling at them and at each
other—I don't know how I slept through it as long as I did.

Massa Jamie took me to a big yard. A man came out to see
who brung him what at this time of night. They talked about
how gimpy I was. Massa ended it by saying, "Well, see what you
can do," kinda leaving it up in the air. Then he gave the man a
key and was gone without a goodbye to me or nothing.

The auction boss took me by the shoulder, but with my bad
foot and good foot manacled together, I couldn't move much.

"Well, hell's bells," he said, inserted the key, and set my
feets free as could be.

I looked down at my ankles, raw from the cuffs.

None too happy at having me unchained, he cuffed me a
good one across the ear. "Get moving!" he said and roughed me
up as he pushed me along.

We stopped in front of a big fence. Behind it metal clanked
and voices whispered. That all stopped when he picked a key on
a huge key ring and opened the gate.

Firelight reflected off hundreds of faces looking at us, faces
just like the ones I left back home that very day. But these faces
didn't cry or smile or nothing. It was like they were dead, they
were so still. People sat or stood. Some had laid themselves on
the ground to sleep. Nothing stirred except the fire twitching
this way and that and a few coughs here and there.

He shoved me into the yard, clanged the gate shut behind
me, locked it, and walked away—and still none of them moved.
They studied me and I them. And then, everybody went back
to what they were doing before the interruption, and I was all
alone in a sea of darkies.

That is, everybody went back to their business except for
one big, big one. Biggest I ever seen, before or since—almost

seven feet tall—not long and spindly like some, but big and beefy with a mean look to his eye. He stepped forward and looked me up and down, seen my foot, but kept that look as he came over to me. For my part, I gots to say I gave him his look right back. When he got real close, I'm a-looking up at him and he's a-looking down at me, as eye to eye as we could get.

Then, the craziest thing happened. While the rest of him stayed big and tough for all to see, his mean eyes softened like a baby's and a right nice smile showed through them. I don't think it was cause I was a weakling. He smiled cause I didn't back down, no matter how big he was. Then he turned and went back to the shadows where he came from. I found myself a corner in the dirt and lay down to wait.

Before dawn, they rounded us up and chained us men together at the hands and around our necks. Heavy ropes bound the women to each other, and the children, taken to a separate line, screamed for their mamas in all kinds of languages.

Don't matter where children come from, they all want their mamas.

They chained me behind the big man from the night before. As we began to move, he looked over his shoulder at me.

"Hmph," he snorted.

I stood tall.

"Looks like we bound to be together," he said, then laughed at his joke.

The crack of a whip snapped our heads around.

"Shut up! All of you."

"Dumb fucks, anyway," he muttered.

"Reynolds," hissed a woman in a pink scarf standing in the line next to us, "you gonna get us all in trouble."

"Girl, you don't think you in trouble now?" he asked, and laughed again.

The tip of a whip caught his shoulder, leaving a big red welt. Reynolds didn't flinch, but he was quiet after that.

Shopkeepers at the market square arrived with goods to sell. We—the human goods—waited by the auction block, watching the start of the day that would decide our destinies.

Men from around the county pulled up in riding traps, ready to haul away new slaves. They came over to where we stood and looked us over. Some opened our mouths and pushed our lips back to see our gums and teeth.

One man looked Reynolds over like he was a horse, turning him this way and that. "Bend down," he said.

Reynolds gave him a look.

"Bend down, I say."

Reynolds wasn't gonna bend over for nobody.

"Boy," said the boss-man who put me in the yard the night before, "the man says to bend over."

Reynolds turned around, his chain pulling at my neck. Slowly, he bent away from the man.

"What are you doing, boy?" asked the customer.

Reynolds stood up and turned to face the man, mixed up. So was the slave master.

"I want to see your scalp," the man said.

Reynolds turned around and lowered his head. The man searched a comb through Reynolds' hair, looking for critters.

"Good enough," the customer said. "Stand up."

Suddenly, Reynolds got real testy, cause the man went to feel Reynolds's johnson. The rest of us looked at each other. So far, no other slave had been touched that way.

Reynolds spat in the man's face. The customer jumped back and a whip cracked.

"Here now," shouted the slave master.

Bright as the new red stripe glowed on his cheek, Reynolds's eyes gleamed even brighter. Reynolds would have it in for this man if he bought him. I knew it. So did the others.

The customer eyed him with an answering gleam. "A strong, mean one, eh?" It wasn't really a question. "There's treatment for that kind of behavior, you know," he warned. He turned to the slave master. "That will bring his price down. I'll let this be known among all the buyers. He's worthless till he's trained."

"Dirty bastard," Reynolds said under his breath as the man walked away. "No man touches me like that and lives to tell it."

Another crack of the whip missed its mark, but Reynolds fell silent.

Turns out it was regular for customers to look over the women even closer than the men. The right pretty ones got lots of attention. That they were up for sale invited mauling from men who wanted nothing more than a quick feel.

Nobody looked at my teeth. One glance at my foot and on they went.

Maybe I won't get sold, I thought, happy at first. Then, not so happy. *If not, what will happen?*

Just before the auction, they let us go to latrine holes. Then it was time. A man in a big black hat and coat climbed up on the block, now surrounded by people in the market for human flesh. One by one, they shoved us up the steps onto a wooden platform and the calling began.

A light-skinned girl with big sad eyes went for more than the rest of us would go for put together, to an elderly man with a leer in his eye.

Then it was Reynolds's turn. They unlocked the chain between me and him. His hands still manacled, he climbed the steps and stood proud.

"Now then. What's the first bid for this fine young speci-men?" asked the auctioneer.

The Cock-Feeler turned to the men around him. "You mean this insolent, defiant, arrogant boy? This is the one I was telling you about, fellas, the one that spat in my face."

"Hey now, he speaks fine English though, don't you, boy?" asked the auctioneer.

Reynolds looked out above their heads and didn't answer.

"I don't hear nothing," said a heckler. "Maybe he's mute!"

"Been on a good Southern plantation all his life—no train-ing needed," answered the auctioneer, then began his mumbo-jumbo.

"No training, my eye," taunted the Cock-Feeler. "I'd like to see you get him to do anything for you right now."

One of the auction men with a whip walked up to Reynolds and pushed his left shoulder with it to turn him around.

"This-here boy will stud your ladies and bring you hand-some young'uns," said the auctioneer.

Reynolds spat at him. Grumbling welled up from the group. Out of nowhere a whip cracked.

Then a man in a light suit outside the cluster of buyers said, "I'll give you one thousand dollars."

So much for talking down Reynolds to lower the price. I'd been listening to the bids for the others, each beginning at a few hundred and ending above a thousand—but none had started there.

The auctioneer babbled on. Hands holding numbered paddles flew up one at a time, then the bidding got fierce. Finally, it came down to the first bidder and the Cock-Squeezer. Guess who won, paying more than two thousand buckaroos?

I wondered if he'd get his money's worth.

All eyes were on Reynolds as they moved him off the stage, poking him with sticks. Nobody wanted to get too close, excepting, of course, his new owner.

Reynolds flashed a look at me as we passed on the steps.

It was my turn.

CHAPTER 9

1862

SOLD

You'll see it all come to pass just like the Bible says,
but in a way you never expected.
—J. Johnson

I was hot and hungry and didn't know whether to look
friendly or not. Reynolds hadn't looked friendly and look how
they fought over him and who won. I couldn't decide, so I
didn't wear any look at all.

After seeing Reynolds, looking at the likes of me was no
treat for the buyers. You could tell by the way their eyes followed him through the crowd, while nobody even looked at me
up there on the block.

Maybe that ain't all bad, I thought. *Might get off easy.*

If nobody bought me, though, would I go back to that yard
where we stayed last night without food and no place to sleep?

I perked myself up, looking off into the distance the way
Reynolds did.

Didn't make no difference. Nobody noticed.

Gloating after his last deal, the auctioneer soured when he seen the next one up for sale. His work cut out for him, he dug right in. "Well now," he began, "what do I hear for this next young man?"

A couple of men turned away.

"Do I hear five hundred?" The auctioneer filled the silence with a collection of budda-bees and budda-bays.

No interest.

He brung the price down, but everybody looked past me at what was coming next. When he came down to three-fifty, an old fellow not as well dressed as the others pushed his way to the front. His long gray hair stuck out all over the place.

"One hundred dollars," he said.

Caught off-guard by the low price, the auctioneer looked over at the manager. You could hardly see the answering nod.

"Sold!" said the auctioneer without even a "going once" or "going twice," and I was down on the ground, following my new owner.

He paid at a table and was given the key to my cuffs. Then he led me to his riding trap—not much more than a wagon, really. I had trouble getting up on it with my hands bound. Without a word, he unlocked them.

Never in my life did I really think about what it would be like to be free—till he unlocked those cuffs. I looked around at the busy crowd, picturing what might happen if I ran. He'd call out and they'd have me on the ground in a horse's shake. I got into the wagon.

Didn't take long to get to his place. He pulled the trap behind a row of small houses on a tiny street and into a little stable.

"All right, help me with this horse," he said as he got out of the wagon. I never took care of a horse in my life, but I seen them cared for and knew how to unhitch her. We got her brushed and watered and in for the night.

"You'll stay in my house," he said.

I never slept overnight in nothing better than a slave shack. Now I was gonna sleep in this-here man's house?

"Your room's down from mine. Never go to bed before me, but always get up before me and have warm water waiting in the basin every morning."

I hobbled behind him through the back door and into a little kitchen.

"You cook?" he asked.

Watching Mama cook was mighty different from watching stable hands with the horses. I shook my head.

"Didn't think so." He put on an old apron. "Well, you're going to learn. Get me that old pan hanging over the sink."

I handed it to him.

"Now, get me that big spatula over there."

I didn't know what a spatula was.

"A pancake turner."

I handed it to him.

So went the preparation for my first meal away from my mama. I cut up carrots and potatoes that we boiled. When dinner was ready, he pointed to two tin plates and I brung them over. He loaded one up good. The other, he loaded up fair. He grabbed a fork and put both plates on the table. I started towards the lesser portion, but he beat me to it, sat down and turned to me.

"What are you waiting for?" he asked.

I hurried to pick up a fork and sat down at the other place—the one with the big portion. I hadn't eaten since I'd been in the fields the day before. It wasn't the hungriest I would be in my life, but I was hungry enough.

The old man bent over his food and picked at it like he didn't care for it. Wasn't like Mama's, but it was good.

A second later, I slowed my chewing and watched him pick at his food. *I am eating at the table of a white man*, I thought.

"Something the matter?" the old man asked.

I shook my head and went back to chewing fast as I could, finishing up in short order.

"Want more?"

I nodded. He waved his hand toward the stove, and I got more and wolfed it down. That night's meal was the best ever, cause I could have all I wanted.

"All right, all right," he said when I was done. "Didn't they feed you today?"

I shook my head.

"You dumb?" He thought I was stupid.

I just looked at him.

"Don't you talk?"

"Yes, sir. I can talk."

"Well then. What's your name?"

"Jacobs, sir."

"Jacobs, huh. Sure it's not Jacob?"

"No sir. That was my daddy's name."

"So you were named after your daddy? Then your name's Jacob."

"No sir. I'm Jacobs cause I belonged to my daddy, Jacob."

"So . . . you'd be . . . Jacob*son*, then."

"Yes, sir. I'm Jacob's son."

"What's your first name?"

I fidgeted with my shirt. "Sir, I already done told you my name. It'd be Jacobs."

"Doesn't make sense, but we'll let it go." The old man studied me like I was some book he never read.

"So, Jacobs," he said in his little old voice. He frowned at my feets.

I pulled them under my chair—not that he could have missed the twist. I'm not saying I liked the man or cared what he thought, but did I want to go back to that auction and change the fact that I ate *what* he did, *when* he did, and *where* he did? No sir.

"First thing we must do is get you some decent shoes."

So he been frowning all this time at the wrappings and not at my feets?

"How'd your foot get that way?"

I thought of the talk Henry had with Mama outside the window about how it happened. Who knew? Shrugging, I said, "Just always been like this. Born this way, is what my mama told me."

He picked up a pipe, filled it, and lit it. "You get around pretty well in spite of it, I see. Hear you were a field hand."

He says I get around all right. I sat up a bit taller and nodded.

"Well, I s'pose I'd better introduce myself. My name is Forrest Tate."

I looked at him kinda funny. Nobody never introduced hisself to me before.

"I'll be straight out about this," said Mr. Tate. "I've got little use for a field hand. My work is keeping numbers straight, but I find myself constantly short of time and in need of someone to run errands." He looked at my foot and cleared his throat. "Another thing. I get so danged caught up in work that the rest of life gets out of hand. I need someone to tidy up the place, keep the cupboards stocked, and look after things."

The place was shy of good housekeeping, but I was no houseman. No sirree Bob.

"I still need to get out to meet with clients and get reports back to them, though." Seemed like he spoke more to hisself now. "Don't know how to get it all done, even with new help," he said, like he forgot I was there.

In a flash though, he was back—and different. "Boy!" His voice carried new strength. "There are dishes to be done!"

I grabbed his dishes and mine.

"Get those clean and put away, then report to me."

"Yes, sir."

He shuffled into another part of the house that began to glow as he lit the lamps.

What a strange little man. One minute, I'm his friend. The next, his slave. Then I smiled. *No different from Massa Jamie.*

Turns out, the man could do nothing for hisself. How he got on before I came along, I didn't know—that is, till later that week when I answered a knock at the door.

"Oh!" An old lady stepped back and teetered on the step's edge. Catching herself, she smoothed her skirts, drew in a breath, and asked, "Is Mr. Tate in?"

I went to get Mr. Tate, who was in the office hunched over his numbers as usual. When he came to the door and seen a lady still standing on his step, he ushered her in, apologizing, then turned to me.

"Jacobs, you must learn your manners."

"Yes, sir."

"I'm sorry, Mrs. Dowling," he said. "It's Jacobs's first week and he's yet to learn the ins and outs of being a gentleman's gentleman."

A what?

"Well, Mr. Tate," said Mrs. Dowling as she sat down on the edge of a loveseat in the parlor, "I'm glad to see you've found someone to help you." She looked me up and down.

I backed into the shadows near the window curtains.

She looked back at Mr. Tate. "I guess you could say Edwina just worked herself to death."

Mr. Tate wiped his spectacles with a handkerchief from his back pocket. "Mrs. Dowling, Edwina had it good here. It was just her time."

"Your sister worked very hard, Mr. Tate. We all watched her go downhill, bless her soul." She sighed and looked around the room. "Place doesn't look the same without her."

Mr. Tate's face got tight, and he stood. "With Jacobs here, it will be back in shape in no time."

Taking his cue, she stood, then glanced at my foot a second time. I backed right into those dusty old curtains.

"Well, Mr. Tate, I came to convey my condolences. If ever you need something, please don't hesitate to ask."

"That's most kind of you, Mrs. Dowling, but I assure you I'm fine now. Good day." The door closed with a bang.

He turned and came for me. He lifted his arm and I readied myself for a thrashing, but he laid it across my shoulder instead—we were about the same height—and took me into his confidence like partners in crime. "When someone comes calling, look through the peephole. Then hightail it back to tell me who it is *before* you open it."

The man was a nutcase.

"All those church ladies want is to get me back into church. That sister of mine hounded me to her dying day about attending. Said I'd rot in hell if I didn't. No more church ladies, hear?"

I nodded.

He was a weak, puny sort with a pointy chin and pince-nez spectacles perched on his big nose. Didn't pay no attention to what he wore or ate, but couldn't stop playing with numbers and what they meant. Must have been good at them cause he worked many nights till the tallow ran down the candlestick. He'd look up, surprised when the wick went out—a kind of timepiece telling him that it must be near midnight. Candles burnt about eight hours, so if he lit one at four . . .

I'd been around the Big House on the plantation enough to know how to wipe cupboards and tables and sweep floors. And I sure knew how to do laundry—yes I did—and in a short time learned to fix simple meals.

One day, I came into his office to announce dinner and found him in a snit.

"Where the devil . . ." He looked up. "Jacobs, what is it?"

"Dinner, sir."

"Yes, yes. Dinner, dinner, dinner. We must have our dinner, mustn't we? While I can't find this blithering receipt. Mr. Whithers will have my hide and kick me out the door if I don't return with all of his . . ."

My eye fell to a crumpled piece of paper on the floor by the desk. I picked it up. "This it, sir?"

"What?" He glanced at it, then went back to pushing papers on his desk. "No, no, no. It's addressed to Mr. Whithers at the top. Saw it only a minute ago. A receipt for . . ."

I touched a little piece of paper on the desk. "Here's one addressed to Mr. Whithers."

He snatched it out of my hand and looked at it. "That's it! Where did you find it, boy?"

"On top of this-here stack of papers, sir. I seen Mr. Whithers's name and . . ."

"I must have set it aside . . ." He stopped and looked at me real slow. "You say you saw . . . What was it you just said, boy?"

"I seen Mr. Whithers's name at the top and . . ."

"You *saw* his *name?*"

"Why, yes, sir. I seen . . ."

"You mean . . . you can *read?*"

"Uh . . ." *Damn.* Slaves who could read caused trouble. We weren't supposed to know nothing. "Sorry, sir . . . I didn't mean to . . ."

"Boy," he stood and came round the desk, "are you telling me you can *read?*"

I backed off as he came at me.

Then he laughed aloud. "Oh ho!" he cried out with joy and danced around the desk. "What a catch I have here! And at what price! Lord, I'd trade a foot for a reader any day of the week!" Grabbing my hands, he made me dance too—gimpy foot and all!

And that's how I moved up from being a houseman to being a bookkeeper's secretary.

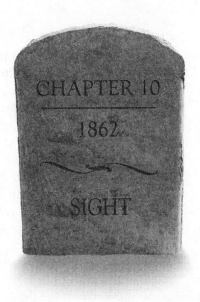

CHAPTER 10

1862

SIGHT

Do something. Make a difference.
—J. Johnson

My writing wasn't up to my reading, and I sure as hell couldn't figure numbers. Numbers were his business. Mine was to match things like I did that first time—searching through papers to find what went with what. We worked out a way where he put a list next to a box of receipts and I'd match them up with it.

After he got used to having me work by his side, he began taking me to business meetings. We got to be a kind of team. He'd hold out his hand for a paper, and I'd have it ready. He'd talk about some point on a chart, and I'd be there with backup work from a folder.

I got to see what life was like in other houses and businesses, nodding at servants as we walked in. I learned from receipts that some servants didn't belong to the houses they worked in. Instead, they were hired from other owners. Others were called "freemen"; they had earned their freedom but worked for the massa just the same to make a living.

Didn't matter if the massa had their papers or not, he still owned them. The only difference was how you framed it.

One night, I cleaned up after supper then put tea on for the two of us. I took it in to find Mr. Tate asleep, his glasses atop a pile of papers. They needed cleaning, so I polished them up.

Checking to make sure the spots were out of them, I noticed something else. As I looked down through Mr. Tate's glasses, dots on the *i*'s and crosses on the *t*'s stood out like never before. I slipped on those spectacles and looked at the papers on his desk. Picking one up, I found I could read it by candlelight, something I could never do since reading in Miss Emily's closet.

I didn't hear Mr. Tate stir till I looked up to see him staring at me.

"Well, boy, it's about time we got you some glasses then, don't you think?"

My smile showed my teeth to him for the first time, yes, it did. Didn't know it was possible to see so good.

After that, I got to be working late into the night just like Mr. Tate. In the daytime, we met clients at their homes or offices. Evenings, we did our bookwork—me matching and him figuring.

"Makes it go faster with you right here when I work," he said. "Better than me putting things off to the side for you to get to later."

Another night, he sat back and fastened his eyes on me. "You'd make a good detective, Jacobs."

This wasn't a bad life.

With all our appointments, I was aware of dates now. A year after I started with Mr. Tate, he and I were to go to the home of a highfalutin railroad tycoon. We rode in the horse trap, our notes and papers in a satchel by Mr. Tate's side. He was to make a proposal about taking on the man's personal account. We got to a very fine home on the edge of town with a grand iron fence that ran clear round his property. The gate man let us in and we rode up a curved drive. Servants took the trap and we climbed the umpteen steps to a front door that opened all by itself.

Oh. A butler stood behind it. "Yes, sir?"

Even in fine clothing, I couldn't mistake that huge muscular figure. I thought he'd be using his muscles out on the land, but no sir, here he was being showed off as he showed us to the massa's office.

My limp gave me away. He looked at me straight-faced like he did when we passed on the auction block. That look spoke of what cannot be described, and he didn't want no pity for it. The man was working at keeping his dignity.

As I looked down at the floor, my eyes passed over my own clothes. Aw, it wasn't nothing like the white folk wore, but for me—a good pair of shoes, breeches, a decent shirt, coat and hat, and a fine pair of spectacles—it wasn't nothing you could snuff at neither. My rank might not be up there with his, but I was respectable and he wasn't, and it shamed me. I don't understand how, but I'm telling you that knowing he was suffering but had a pride that wouldn't show it, and knowing I wasn't suffering and had pride in myself, made it worse. I felt bad for both of us.

What we were had decided what we would be. That, and who took a liking to it. That was the key. His good looks and big muscular frame made him a toy or a workhorse. I was gimpy but could read. That second part made me valuable. But both of us were ashamed cause neither of us had no say in it.

That was the difference between those that got freed and those that didn't. The freed could decide who they wanted to work for. That they would work was a given. Where they would work—would they move to a different place or even a different state or maybe Out West on the frontier?—and what they would do, was up to them. For us slaves, the choosing was out of our hands.

It was a big difference, and we both felt it. Pain, hatred, and burnt pride oozed off Reynolds and into me as we followed him down the hallway. His troubles were my own. My next owner might be his owner, and what could I do about it? I never craved freedom before this, but now it started working on me.

After that day, I would never be the same.

Reynolds's master came in after we'd been in the library a few minutes. Servants brung tea for him and Mr. Tate while I stood behind my boss, ready with the papers he needed.

I wasn't as sharp as usual.

"Jacobs! Wake up! Get out the plan we worked on last night."

I snapped out of it real quick.

J. Robert Townsend sat back in his chair and looked me over. "I remember that boy from the auction," he said. His eyes narrowed as he sized me up.

"And a fine specimen your butler has become," said Mr. Tate.

"Ah, you don't know the half of it," twinkled Townsend. He leaned closer and winked at Mr. Tate, who drew back and shuffled his papers, harrumphing and ahem-ing in a state of embarrassment I'd never seen in a white man. Townsend looked up to see if I caught the drift. I met his eye, hatred in mine.

"I see that yours has the same spirit as my butler," said Townsend.

"This boy can read," said Mr. Tate.

Townsend put down his drink. "You don't say." He gave me a second glance and dismissed me again.

I didn't see Reynolds no more that day. Townsend showed us to the door, and that was that.

That night I lay wondering what I would choose to do for a living if I had the right. Wanting to prove my manhood, I might go back to the fields. But I did get a lot out of working for Mr. Tate, showing that a man of color could be an asset to anyone of any color. I settled down and told myself I'd probably choose what I was already doing anyhow. Made it easier to sleep at night.

If I had known I'd get the chance to make that choice very soon, I might not have slept so well. No sirree Bob. I probably wouldn't have slept at all.

Mr. Tate began letting me make runs without him—not to appointments, but to carry messages, make deliveries, or post a letter.

One day, I had to pick up receipts he needed from Mr. Townsend. Looking forward to seeing Reynolds, I gave the door knocker a thump or two, but nobody came.

A little old gardener ran from around the side, a finger to his lips. "You don't want to disturb Mr. Townsend now."

"There's something he must do," I said. "Is he in?"

"Mm-hmm. He be in. But I ain't bothering him, and you'd best not either." He ran back around the way he came out.

I turned back to the door and got testy with the knocker. Reynolds answered, his shirt half in and half out, his face all sweaty. Not a good time to be talking about receipts, I could tell.

His eyes were mean. "What you want?"

"I can see now's not the t—"

"The hell it ain't!" Reynolds turned away but left the door open. "Townsend," he yelled back into the house. "You got yourself a right pretty visitor." He turned back and glared at me as Mr. Townsend came down the stairs.

"He's all yours," said Reynolds as Townsend, just as untidy but with combed hair, came to the door.

My stomach in knots, I explained the reason for my unscheduled call.

"Boy," said Mr. Townsend, "you sure you got to have those papers right now?"

I got the receipts all right, but I also got a dirty look from Reynolds who stayed in the background, watching me out of the corner of his eye. He didn't want nobody knowing what I guessed and that made us both nervous. I left and never went back.

Them church ladies never came back to Mr. Tate's neither. His routine stayed the same no matter what day it was. I cooked and cleaned and laundered and ran errands and did the marketing so he could stay at home running his figures, day and night.

Each day, I bumped into others out running for their massas and began seeing some of the same faces. Mr. Tate even let me take the trap all by myself when I had to go more than a mile or two on my run. Got me feeling what it would be like to be on my own or working as a bondsman. In seven years, I could be free. I tried pretending I was free now, just to see what it felt like. But there was no way to know. I couldn't even guess.

From conversations with other slaves, I learned a lot about what was going on in the rest of the world.

"Old Mr. Joseph's finally joining up," Mac from the village pantry told me one day as we waited in the colored line at the postal station.

"Sad about Jason Avery," said someone in front.

"Sure is," said Mac. He turned to me. "Mr. Avery—you know, the fella who fixes shoes?"

I'd been to the shoe repair and nodded.

"His son came home in a box, day before yesterday."

Fella in front of Mac spoke to me. "We still winning though," he said and smiled.

Another day, Mac cocked his head to signal me. He walked behind a store, and I followed. A bunch of coloreds listened close to a young boy from a house farther uptown.

". . . they found him across the river and over a couple of counties," the boy said.

The crowd groaned.

"Dragged him back and put him in a stall all by hisself with only water for seven days."

"Nobody caught Pearl?"

"Nope. Looks like she got away."

They nodded at each other.

One day, Mac pulled me over to the side of the walk.

"I ain't gonna be seeing you no more," he said, and I knew he was packing to go.

"Seen them Smith folks last night?" I asked.

People right in town and others just north of here took in runaways, then sent them on to others. It was like a chain all the way North. Once you crossed into Ohio, you were free.

Free!

He nodded. "They got it all fixed up."

"Well, good luck."

He looked at me, both fear and triumph shining in his eyes. Never did hear of him again. Maybe he made it.

Just after the first of the year in '63, everybody began making a fuss over Mr. Lincoln's Emancipation Proclamation that said there wouldn't be no more slaves in rebel states.

We gathered that day behind the inn, listening to the news from another slave that could read. I didn't want them to know I could read. They might think I was stepping out from where I belonged.

"We's free!" everybody said.

"What you talking about?" laughed Jack, a runner for one of the bigger households. "You think the Confederate States of America gonna think that's so?"

I stopped hopping around with everybody and listened.

"We ain't no part of the U.S. of A. now, boy," he said to one of the younger kids that still danced. Then he spoke to the rest of us. "They can't pass laws or proclamations or whatever for the Confederate States no more. We a different country altogether."

Sophie the laundress spoke up. "But if we make it to the North, then we're free!"

Jack laughed. "You think everybody up there's gonna let their slaves go just cause The Man says so?" He shook his head. "That ain't no law. I heard lawyers dining at the inn say, 'That proclamation's only what one man, Abraham Lincoln, says.'"

"But he's president!" shouted Sophie.

"He ain't nothing if the people don't like him."

Later we heard of some who made it all the way north of the Mason-Dixon line, then got caught by slave catchers sent up by the Southern plantations. They had police on the take in the North, which meant everybody had to watch out for The Law up there too. Some Union states had slaves all the way through the War. Slavery wasn't even outlawed in the U.S. of A. till they passed an amendment after the War, in 1865.

Pete from the Thompson house stopped me one day in front of the grocery. "You hear from anyone at your old plantation?"

I shook my head. Made me sad just to think of them.

"I heard old men, women, and children's all that's left at any of them plantations anymore," he said.

Same was true here in town. Fewer and fewer able-bodied men walked about. Only old folk, very young folk, women, and no-good gimpies like me were left. But after a while, even we began to disappear. The old ones signed up. Boys not yet men deserted their homes. Women and children—why, whole families—vanished. Made a person wonder why you kept doing what you did if so many others didn't. Made you wonder too whether the slaves that ran away made it.

We heard about some that didn't. Too valuable to be hanged, their owners put them to hard labor or cut off an ear to make the rest pay attention. Even so, plantations were wearing down with no men to run them.

In town, the women—busy trying to keep things going and make ends meet—didn't look so pretty and dressed up like they used to. They began dwindling in numbers too. Most closed up shop and left to stay with relatives someplace else. Lots of empty homes were mixed in here and there, while others bulged with females and not-so-young children. I heard of whole towns clearing out.

Mr. Tate's clientele changed with the times. More and more of his clients were females, which kept him busier than ever since most weren't schooled to figure at all.

Things between us went pretty smooth, though. He knew his business, and I got mine down good too. Not much passed between us cause we kept so busy.

One morning, I got his tea ready to take into his office, like always. Even before I got there, I felt something amiss. He wasn't there. I went upstairs to find him stiff in his bed. The man done kicked the bucket.

Didn't take me but two seconds to know what to do. I scooted down the front stairs and up the back stairs to get my belongings. Wrapping them with some cheese and biscuits in a scarf, I pulled the corners together and tied it up real good, then put more food in my—well, in Mr. Tate's—valise. Lickety-split, I was out the back door, my valise at my side like it was just another day. But it wasn't.

Today was Freedom Day.

CHAPTER 11

1863

ESCAPE

People live like they feel Shadows around them all the time.
—J. Johnson

I hitched the horse to the trap and skedaddled like I was late to meet a client. Farther from our little neighborhood, people started to look at me funny, so I slowed down, nodding here and there, but that wouldn't wash for long. An unknown colored like me would be cause for suspicion on horseback; one driving a trap was sure cause for alarm.

I got more and more uncomfortable. Soon as I found a spot, I parked the trap, tied up the horse, and gave her some oats to keep her quiet a while. Then I got outta there, strolling along the sidewalk like I belonged. Held my head no higher than any other day, looking like I had business on my mind yet glad to see the sunshine—you know—nodded at other coloreds, looked down from meeting eyes with the whites, just like usual. I wasn't dressed up in no suit or nothing, just my regular pants and shirt—respectable for a slave. I thanked the Lord my new shoes were broken in.

As I walked farther and farther from Mr. Tate's, the looks I got told me I'd become a stranger. My limp brought stares and the tied-up scarf was telltale. Add to that, a colored you didn't know, and it didn't bode no good at all.

I couldn't keep this up, so I found a park in a town square and got me a drink from a pump. Sitting at a bench, I opened the scarf and had me a biscuit. Early morning, there weren't many in the park yet. Mothers and mammies with babies and little children wouldn't be out so soon. Wasn't like the hot time of year when everybody got things done outside before the worst heat of the day.

I tucked everything from the scarf I could into the valise. Standing up, I patted it shut and hoofed it over to a stand of trees. I stashed what wouldn't fit in my valise under some brush. After checking to see if anybody was looking, I slid between the bushes and into the brush myself.

I crawled as close to the center of the grove as I could. Laying on my belly, I shoved my valise under another big heavy bush, then rolled over to meet it. Leaves brushed against my face. Bees buzzed in blossoms farther up, but down here it was cool and quiet.

My clothes ruined now, I couldn't play at doing regular business no more. Besides, if anyone stopped me, my valise would tell the story. I would have to do my moving at night. Wasn't no other way.

The day unfolded as I listened. Children's voices rang, their mammies calling for them to be careful as they ran around on the nearby green.

I had to make water, so when things quieted, I rolled out from under my bush to where I could see sky. Late morning— the picnickers hadn't yet arrived, but the morning visitors had gone home. Finishing my business, I returned to my spot and waited out the day.

I woke to the sound of sniffing close by, took a look and, wouldn't you know, me and a terrier were eye to eye. He growled and backed away, then barked.

"Come here, Sparky," called a woman.

"Git away," I whispered, flicking at it with my fingers. But the critter wasn't leaving.

"Sparky, where are you?" called the voice, closer now.

I froze.

"Sparky!" She was real close. "Get out of those bushes. You'll get all dirty." Arms reached in. Pretty white hands grabbed a ferocious Sparky, pulling him—barking all the while—away.

The rest of the afternoon was downhill except for my appetite. At one point I was so hungry, I just had to slide out a little so's I could get myself a piece of cheese. Didn't have no water—another mistake. Could have easily brung a jug.

Now that I thought about it, I didn't have to leave quite so fast. Nobody would have known Mr. Tate died. Far as I could remember, he didn't have no appointments today.

I thought about going back and stocking up better, but how could I carry more? No sir, I'd move on and find food and water as I went.

After dark, I rolled out from under the bush. Seeing no one, I began to move, staying close to the brush. A fugitive now, my movements were no longer open and "how-you-all-doing." No, sir. Didn't want to see nobody, especially no dogs. Even if nobody seen you, if there's a dog around, he'll let everyone know you're there.

I moved along the backs of houses to get out of the main part of town, trying not to take too many turns, cause I sure didn't want to be going south. Pulling vegetables as I went, I ate, grabbed more for my pockets and moved on, running as best I could. I knew from my travels with Mr. Tate that there weren't but seven miles of real city before I would be in the country.

If I didn't make it and got caught, who would they return me to? Mr. Tate was dead. What would they do with a gimp like me?

I had to make it. I just had to.

Hiking faster than ever, I stopped at a pump or two for water. My bad ankle, strong as it was, got sore and after a while wouldn't let me alone. Hobbling down one dark alley, I found a big tree branch, broke it in half and used it to help me get out of town.

Fences lined the road now for farms with animals or nice country houses. I moved off the road to get away from the homes with their dogs and into fields for more vegetables. Skulking around outside one barn, I looked around the corner and seen a smokehouse, its door half open. Peering in, didn't I see a big old ham just a-hanging there for anyone to take, but too big for just me. A knife on a plank table gleamed in the moonlight streaming in through a little window. Swift as I could, I cut me a hunk. Tearing it in pieces, I ate some, stuffed the rest into my pockets, and turned to go.

Took me for a fright—a man stood like a statue in the doorway. Couldn't tell if he was black or white, but he was big, that was for sure. He must have been my color. Had to be, else why wasn't he out fighting?

He came towards me. I backed up. I seen some who been caught red-handed and knew what they did when that happened. Took your hand right away, yes they did.

Oh Lordy, one-handed and a bad foot to boot.

He reached for me and I backed up far as I could.

"You gonna want this," said a big black voice. I could see his eyes now in the moonlight. In his hands was a big chunk of bread.

I took—grabbed—it, I'm afraid. And I was. Afraid. Wasn't thinking about being nice or nothing, just about getting caught. Even though he gave me bread, he could be loyal to the family that fed him.

"Thanks," I sputtered.

He grabbed a leather bag off a nail on the side wall. "And this, for your eats."

I slung it over my shoulder.

"How long you been running?" he asked.

"Just since this morning."

"You from here then?"

"In town," I answered. Relaxing just a hair, I started babbling. "My boss, he up and died this morning, and I skedaddled before anybody knew."

He stood, looking at me.

Realizing what he might be thinking, I said, "I didn't kill him. No sir. Just found him dead in bed, natural as could be."

I was talking too much. Once word got out about Mr. Tate, everybody would be on the lookout for you-know-who.

"What else you need?" This man was gonna help me. Maybe he wanted to come hisself but couldn't cause of a wife or family or who knows what.

"I ain't got nothing to hold water."

He disappeared. After a while, I got itchy standing in that shack, my pockets full of meat just hucked from that-there ham. Red-handed indeed.

He was back. "Take this. Best I could find." He handed me a good tin canteen with a twist cap and shoulder strap. "Now git. Don't tell nobody you was here or that I helped you."

I tried to thank him.

"Git outta here," he hissed.

I ran out the door.

Oh Lordy, Lordy, Lordy! I thought. *Thank you, Lord, for sending me to this-here place.*

Just as I was praising the Lord, a dog from the house up and howled like a hunting hound. A window slammed shut, and I ran. Oh yes I did.

My gait evened up with that old stick, and I didn't stop for nothing all night, except once to fill my canteen at a watering hole. Cutting across fields and through woods and up hills and down through streams and across the land, I moved fast as I could go, scared silly of being close to the city. It was easy to trip in the weeds with my wobbly foot and my stick cane, so I watched every step. Couldn't afford to get hurt. Had to keep use of what the good Lord gave me.

Much later, things got easier to see. A new day dawned and I found another hiding place by a crick in the middle of a big old woods. I'd be good here till evening when I'd do it all over again. Had no idea how far I was or how far I had to go. I ached all over but didn't pay it no attention. My body would get used to it. Had to.

I had no other choice.

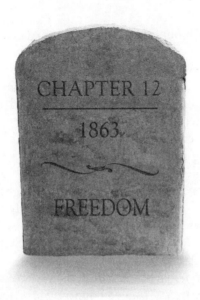

CHAPTER 12

1863

FREEDOM

You are each angels—earth angels—there to help each other.
—J. Johnson

Now, I could tell you about each and every day on my trek north. Yes, I could. Over here where I am now, we don't rely on brain cells to keep track of what happened. No sirree. We got another system of remembering on This Side. I don't know how it works, but it sure is different from when you're living. We can remember every little detail, zoom in and zoom out, and speed things up or slow them down. We can play them over and over and skip ahead if we want, which is what we gonna do right now, seeing as how I got so much to say and time's a-wasting—least it is for you-all. Over here, well, time just ain't the same. Let's just leave it at that.

Over the next fortnight or so, I made my way north of Alabama and into Tennessee. Ran into others like me and heard that it worked better if you headed northeast, so that's the way

I went, skirting mountains that run from Alabama on up eastwards.

I also heard where to stop and where not to. My first stop in Tennessee, the home dweller gave me a map of what was ahead. The lantern light in his cellar showed a shadow-line meant to be a river on the cloth map.

"It'll be easier if you follow the rivers and lowlands, see," he said, showing me.

I had a problem with going the easiest way. "Anyone trying to catch a person like me would know that, right?"

"I suppose so," he said, like he wasn't really sure. "Be careful. Border states like Kentucky still have slaves."

"Far as I'm concerned, they're all Slave States till I cross that river into Ohio."

From then on, instead of taking the easy route, I hightailed it through some pretty rugged country. Surprised me, though. In some ways, it was easier. People in the hills took kindlier to someone showing up at their barn in early evening. Knew what you was about soon's you showed up, took you right in and told you how far to go and where to stop before morning. Further I drew north, the more often this happened. Stay to the hills, I learned, if you wanted to see a friendly face.

Cutting over to eastern Kentucky, I was even more welcomed. I even heard of a Kentucky regiment of coloreds up north a ways that fought Confederates. But Kentucky was still borderline. I wouldn't quit till I crossed the Ohio.

The night before getting there, we stopped at a resting spot several days north of Lexington. A little group, we had gathered one by one along the way till there were five of us, with no children. I wouldn't travel with children. Hard enough to move at my own pace. Slowing down for a family just didn't suit me. I wasn't too comfortable traveling with women, neither, but our little group did have a married couple. Hattie, a right tough young thing, kept up with the rest of us just fine.

Course, the strongest and fastest ones traveling our way wouldn't have me for the same reason I didn't want women or children with us. We had us a picking order—you picked who you wanted when you came across them, but they might not want you. Wasn't simple but it worked, and we all passed information back and forth. We learned what was to come and showed where we'd all been. It wasn't lonely but it wasn't easy, and it was definitely dangerous.

My night traveling idea seemed to be the way. Anybody stupid enough to travel by day didn't make it this far. We stayed off roads and kept to main paths that might have been started off by deer or Injuns but by now were well trampled. There were signs along the paths too, but not ones just anybody could read. You had to know the signals and codes.

Hattie and Maxwell joined me when we found ourselves together in a barn just north of the Alabama state line. Early in the trip, we didn't know who to trust so we slept in piles of straw that day, not saying much. Setting out the next night, we stuck together, since we were going the same way.

There's safety in numbers, but too many draws attention. When we met up with another few the next night, we decided to go on by ourselves at our own speed.

Into Tennessee, our next tagalong joined us. Ralph didn't have no shoes. They gave him some at the stop where we met. How that man loved those shoes! I don't think he ever had a pair before. These weren't boots, mind you. They were shoes, and they rubbed and chafed his toes and heels so, he had to take them off after about an hour.

"You gotta break them in slow," said Maxwell.

The man told him that when he gave Ralph the shoes, but I guess he didn't listen. That was the thing about Ralph. He didn't listen.

The last one joined our group in the hills close to Kentucky. Quiet and good at scouting paths, Girard didn't cause no harm. In fact, he took the lead.

Close to the river, we found our stop just north of Lexington where food awaited. Seemed those fast ones ahead of us told them we were coming behind, so they'd be ready. A man showed us the stairs to the cellar under the house. Lanterns were lit, and a sign downstairs said, "At sundown, someone will tell you about the river." Exhausted, we slept, but I woke up a lot.

Freedom was just ahead!

Late afternoon, a door opened and we heard footsteps. A man and woman carried baskets of food downstairs. We gathered around and took our portions, stowing them and saying thank you, real polite and quiet-like.

The old man sat down on the dirt floor with us and spread out his map. "This is where you are. . . ." We went through the direction-giving.

He folded the map away when we had it in our heads real good. "Now," he said, "when you take the turnoff to the right, stay away from the river. They police the riverfront all the time. Keep the river in sight, though. Know where it is. It winds some and if you lose sight of it, you'll get lost."

We nodded.

"You need to go about five miles east, and if you're close enough to the river, another path going north will take you to a crossing. You got any money on you?"

We looked at each other. I had a few pence but wanted to see what they had before I volunteered. I liked my companions, but not so much I wanted them to know I carried coins.

"Well, most don't," he said. "It does help if you give them something. Kind of a gesture, if you know what I mean."

We looked at him, blank-faced.

He went on. "There's a code to say, just like the one you used to get here."

We knew all about codes. Used them whenever we came on a person. Codes weren't good for long. They were always changing.

"'January maple syrup' is the code for this evening." He looked around the group. "You all got that?"

We nodded, and I repeated it. "January maple syrup."

"You'll know the ones who run the crossing by their bandanas. This is Wednesday—red bandana day."

He started to get up. "Oh." He sat back down. "One more thing."

We leaned closer.

"When you get to the other side, be careful."

We frowned. We'd be in Freedom Land. Why'd we have to be careful?

"They got people over there, looking for runaways."

I remembered Jack telling me the same thing back in Alabama. So it was true.

"It happens." He sighed. "You get all the way there, and they bring you all the way back." He looked at us real good. "Just be careful."

A good note for him to leave us on. We been ready to make a big fuss once we got across that-there river.

We didn't have no problem getting to it, though it began to rain. We trod easterly alongside another five miles till we came to the path that led to the crossing, which we found in no time. Near the area on the banks where a beached wooden raft waited, someone came out of the woods, scaring us. Then we seen his red bandana and relaxed.

"Maple syrup in January," I whispered when he was close enough.

That was all he needed. Another came out of the bushes, then another—all wearing red bandanas. He led us to the raft where another group of runaways waited. They motioned for us to get on, then all three pushed the raft out and two carrying long poles jumped on.

We were off! I'll never forget the night I crossed that river. No sirree Bob. Just setting foot on that raft was a thrill. The boy poled us out into the current, and I hung on with my feets, standing quiet like everyone else, watching the land on the north side get closer and closer.

The north bank looked just like the other one, but it wasn't. No sirree, it was not. This-here land was Freedom Land!

I stepped off the raft a free man. My, did we jump and laugh and sing!

"Hush up!" a red bandana reminded us in a loud whisper. "You wanna get us all killed?"

We quit yelling, except for Ralph.

"You ain't safe yet," he said, and Ralph stopped too. "You're gonna give away our new spot." A boy floating back and forth on that river could get into real trouble, maybe even get killed.

He pointed at a hill. "See that path? Take that to the road and go left to the first house. You'll be taken care of there.

Good luck." We shook hands, then the red bandanas were gone, swallowed by the river's rainy darkness.

We hiked up the hill and down the road to the first house next to the river. Window-glow pulled us to a barn where men waited with food and supplies.

"You boys ought to think about volunteering to fight the Rebs," said one, as he poured hot chicken soup straight off the fire.

We stood in line, watching him serve. Sure smelled good. Holding our tins out, we looked at one another to see what we thought about his idea.

In the darkness, I'd noticed one helluva big feller waiting for the raft with the rest of us before we came over. In the lantern light now, I recognized Reynolds. But he didn't look like Reynolds. Seemed meaner and wouldn't look nobody in the eye.

"Over Cincinnati way, they're signing up volunteers for a colored militia," said the white man who passed out soup. "Anybody joining?"

"You mean we get a chance to whup the same Southern ass that whupped us?" I stepped up to the man, standing tall. "Yes sirree, I'll be going for sure."

The soup man caught my limp. His face clouded, then shut down.

I made myself a few inches taller. "Mister," I said, "these two feets got me all the way here from way down in Alabama, now, didn't they?"

At that, Reynolds turned. Though I was only half-shod and bearded, there was no way he couldn't recognize me now.

"Hello, Reynolds," I said. "Been a while, and a ways, I'd say."

He brightened. "Why you're that little . . . You mean to tell me . . ." He stood there putting my story together in half-sentences and began to laugh, then remembered.

His smile disappeared. "Come here, boy."

I walked over, reached way up, and put my hand on his shoulder. "Good to see you," I said and meant it.

"I never gave two licks for you at auction," he said. "But you beat me by a milestone with that master of yours and your reading and such." He jerked away, his face mean again. "You ever so much as whisper what you seen at that bastard's house, I'll kill you. Never tell a soul. Swear it. Now."

Turning, I said, "Reynolds, I don't know what you talking about."

He grabbed my shoulder and turned me back to him. "That's another thing." His lowered voice in a harsh whisper. "I don't go by that name no more. That name is dust, hear?"

"So what do I call you?"

"Call me Roberts."

I nodded and walked over to join the others sitting at a plank table.

Me and Reynolds—Roberts—we just got off on the wrong foot, that's all. And coming from me who's got only one good foot, I don't take that saying lightly. No sirree Bob.

Laughter made me turn around. Roberts was talking to me. "Then you run away and make it here on that foot just like I does on my good big ones?" Laughing again, he said, "If that don't beat all."

He turned to the man rounding up troops. "Yes, sir," he said as he walked over to me, "I'll join that militia, and I can vouch for the worthiness of this man here too." His arm reached across my shoulders. "He can do more than you can shake a stick at. Would you believe this-here man can read?"

A big guy with a cigar hanging out of his mouth walked over. "What'd you say?"

Oh Lordy, I thought. *I'm in for it now.*

Excepting I wasn't no slave no more, was I? I was a free man. I had to get used to that. I was free. Free!

"This-here fella reads and writes with the best of them." Roberts talked bigger than the two of us put together. Just wasn't true. My reading was fair, but my writing and figuring . . .

"What's your name?" the man asked me.

"Jacobs, sir."

"Come over here, Jacobs," he said, leading me to a table lit by a lantern hanging close by. He pulled a slip of paper and a pencil out of his jacket pocket. "What's your first name?"

"Sir, that is my first name. Jacobs. My last name . . ." Now, here was a problem. Most kept their master's last name. I wanted a grand name, a white name, a plain name. A while ago, somebody told me you had to know the president and vice president's names, Lincoln and Johnson, to live in this country. Everybody would be taking the name Lincoln, they told me down South.

"Last name's Johnson."

The man looked at me funny.

"Jacobs Johnson, sir. That's my name."

"Kind of confusing, wouldn't you say?" He looked at Roberts, who shrugged.

"Some folks call me Jeb," I fibbed, "if you like that better." Don't know where that came from, but there it was.

The man nodded. "Jeb Johnson," he wrote. "You say you read and write?"

"Well, now, I ain't gonna say I'm real good at either."

"He worked for a bookkeeper," said Roberts. "Helped with the books and went on calls."

The man looked me over, noting my spectacles.

I pushed them farther up my nose so they'd be less noticeable. I wanted to carry a gun—to shoot and be a man—not write and read the whole time.

"We *need* literate coloreds, Jeb," said the man. He made a few notes and stood. "Report to me in the morning, and we'll get you a job that will suit you just fine. You'll know where to find me."

"Yes, sir," I said and followed Roberts out of the barn to a mess of others forming up. We hiked all night to bivouac just outside Cincinnati on a hill full of pup tents for new recruits in this-here man's army.

"You all don't know how lucky you are," said the man leading us—an officer, it turned out. "Tents just came in. Otherwise you'd be out in the rain like everyone else."

Roberts and I picked a two-man tent up the hill, away from the latrines. We crawled in and lay down on the muddy grass.

I was in the army with Roberts. Would you believe it?

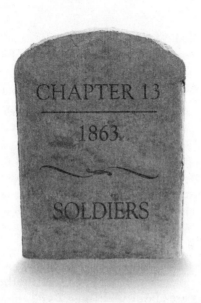

CHAPTER 13

1863

SOLDIERS

There's things you can change.
—J. Johnson

Before dawn, someone called out, waking me. I rolled out of the tent and looked to find us surrounded by hundreds of white tents all over the hills. To the east, cooking fires burned. Men gathered round other campfires, warming their hands.

No one wore a uniform. Noticed that right off.

At the top of our hill, a colored man played reveille. The hills came alive as men crawled out of their tents and lined up in a large circle fifteen or twenty deep round a flagpole at the top of the hill. A sad lineup it was, the men all bedraggled and unshaven. But we were freemen, weren't we! And now we were soldiers!

Are soldiers free? I wondered, but put that question to rest right quick. We were gonna fight Confederates. That was the important part.

Someone yelled, "Ten-hut!"

Everybody stood at attention and saluted. First man I seen in uniform since I got there—a white man with stripes on his shoulders—climbed up the hill. A nonuniformed black playing a drum followed. They reached the top and stopped. The drum rolled, the man saluted like everybody else, including me, and the flag rose to full mast.

The white man turned and faced the rest of us. "Men, some of you have been here a while, and some are new."

I looked around at the others standing at attention, then turned straight ahead like them. *They been here and are still dressed in tatters and sleep on the ground?*

"Some of you just got in last night, I hear."

"They's new ones *every* night," said a man under his breath.

"And we lose others every night," said another.

"Well, things are about to change," said the officer on the hill. "The United States government has just decreed you men fit for military employment, and you shall receive wages."

The men shifted their weight and looked at each other.

"We not already in military employment?" I asked the man to my right.

"Oh, yes, sir, you is in the military," he whispered. "And you is employed. But is you getting paid? And is you free? Those are questions in this-here Black Brigade."

The men mumbled and talked under their breath. They'd heard it before.

The Black Brigade. On my way north, I'd heard how the military gathered them together, forcing coloreds from their homes and breaking up families, to build fortifications to protect the city from attack.

"Thing you don't know," said the fellow next to me, "is that Cincinnati ain't a free city."

I looked at him. "What do you mean it ain't free?"

"You in Cincinnati, you still a slave," he said real hushed now.

"But Cincinnati is in Ohio."

"Don't mean nothing." He looked around. "Things was real bad here in the Brigade. Then they made us regular army and changed commanders." Nobody was paying us any attention, so he went on. "Everybody that left the Brigade came back and brought more with them."

A man next to him shook his head and muttered, "Still, we don't do nothing but dig ditches and clean up after others."

Another in front spoke over his shoulder. "This ain't no army. You see any rifles?"

I looked across the hills at the men, all of them in ratty old shirts and pants that wouldn't hold together in the wind. Roberts stood off to the side, head and shoulders above everybody else, and caught my eye, a wary look in his. The officer at the top of the hill dismissed us. I shrugged in answer to Roberts's look as we moved off to the cook fires for our first army meal.

"But you gots food to eat and you're safe, ain't you?" I asked the first fellow as we fell into step.

"Food's getting scarce," he said as we moved up in line. "We lose a few every night that go looking for something better farther north."

I could see why. The stuff they ladled into my tin was nothing but watered-down porridge. He was right.

I found Roberts. "You hearing what I'm hearing?"

"Don't sound like much of a army," he said. "They might not feed and clothe us. And they might not pay us either." He looked at the men still waiting in line. "Better than the running we been doing, though."

Starved, I supped my porridge to the bottom of my tin.

"Let's wait and see what happens," he said. "I hear they send troops to battle here and there. Some being deployed to Kansas soon. Maybe that'll be us."

Kansas—a mighty long way from Cincinnati, I thought. And we'd just arrived. If the city wasn't friendly to slaves and this was a Free State, how far did we have to go to find a place that *would* welcome us?

"I hear there are ways to get farther north to kinder people that don't hold to slavery at all," said Roberts. "Might hike myself up that way if things don't get better."

I hadn't climbed over hill and dale, tunneled under homes, hid from hounds, slept days and traveled nights just to get myself into a worse sit-yation than what I left. Course, if I stayed at Mr. Tate's, I'd have been sold at auction again for sure. No, this was better. At least I had some choice in this matter. I could always desert.

"They shoot deserters," said Roberts, reading my mind.

"They shoot runaway slaves too," I said. "Didn't stop us."

We stayed and I worked in the commanding officer's tent cause of my reading and also cause of my foot; they didn't think I could be regular army. But when they needed help digging latrines and maintaining fortifications, *that* they thought I could do.

After a few weeks, troop morale got worse. The food didn't get better and portions became less. Stew without meat is soup, at best.

"They're sending out troops to other parts tomorrow," said Roberts one night at supper, "but not us."

It had rained three days straight. High winds made it impossible to keep the tents up and ourselves dry. More and more were sent to the infirmary with dysentery, and I myself got a cough I couldn't get rid of. Plus, I was starving. My clothes hung on me like a scarecrow. Even Roberts looked less like muscle and more like skin and bones.

"I've had it," he said. "We stay long enough, who knows if we'll even get out alive. Listen," he said, his mouth close to my ear, "a few of us are gonna sneak out this evening to round up some rations." He looked at me. "You coming?"

Stealing food—why, I'd done that all the way from Alabama. Found some damn good vittles too.

"I'm with you." Never felt safer than with Roberts at my side. I never told his secret and he never laughed at my gimp. We had an understanding I felt good about. Nothing could go wrong staying with Roberts.

That evening, we lit out of there soon as the sentry passed. Blessed with a cloudy night, ten dark shapes made their way round the side of the hill away from camp. We met up beside a big tree not far from the main highway.

"What we's after is food," said a gruff old guy we all called the General. He'd been in the Brigade since it was only a militia. "We gonna split in two." He divided us up. "You five go round west and see what-all waits in the countryside. We'll go

north and see what's there." With him were me, Roberts, and
two others. The groups started to leave when he called, hushed
but military-like, "Halt!"

Everybody stopped.

"Any of you gets in trouble, we got to have a signal," he
said.

Roberts spoke up. "Don't have to be nothing more than a
birdcall, does it?"

"Birds don't call at night," said the General.

"Some do." Roberts hooted like an owl.

"We gonna hear that?" asked young Andrews from the
other group.

"You gonna hear it," said Roberts, and we were off.

"Halt!"

We stopped again.

"When we gonna meet up?" the General asked

"How 'bout just before daybreak?" said Roberts.

Andrews looked at the sky. "Ain't no moon or nothing to
tell time tonight."

"Fore daylight, we regroup here. Anyone gets something
big or has trouble fore that, call the signal loud and clear and we
all skedaddle back here," said the General.

This time we really *were* off. Staying away from the road,
we made our way over the hills to the first farm not far away.

"Too obvious," said the General. "They'd know it was
someone from the camp."

We moved on. The ground was wet and so were our feets
by the time we came to a smaller farm farther on. Passed that
one by too for the same reason. It began to rain. That didn't
suit us none either, but we didn't turn back. No sir, we were on
a mission.

We walked through the woods Indian-style. "Toe-heel" is
what the General said they did to be quiet. Sure, branches
cracked and we bothered a few coons, but soon we came to a
nice little place smack in the middle of them woods with outbuildings and all. Outbuildings were important cause that's
where the livestock would be, if any was left. Same for hams
and meat hung to dry.

We skirted the perimeter. Lights were out and no dogs barked, thank God. The General motioned me and Roberts to move up to the outbuilding farthest from the house. We checked inside. Farming equipment. Shaking his head, Roberts moved to the next, me right behind. There we found bags of flour and grain—dry goods for our cooks.

That caused a little meeting. The General wanted to take it and go back.

"We take this, what we gonna do with it?" asked Roberts.

"We been doing this since the beginning, boys," said the General. "The cooks act like it was theirs to begin with and make special flatbread or pancakes just for us. They know who brung it. Let's take it."

We hauled those bags on our backs—not more than forty pounds apiece—nothing we couldn't get to camp. We made it to the rendezvous, and Roberts signalled the others in with his bird call. In fifteen minutes, they were back, one with a ham across his shoulders. We lay low as we came around the hill into camp and took our booty to our tents. Wasn't no room left for us inside, but we had food, yes we did.

The General hiked down to the cook's quarters, roused one and told him. Fore we knew it, seven were up to our tents, giving us the nod that we'd be in their good graces. Next morning, we headed to the mess tent and, lo and behold, wasn't there a sort of eggless cornbread that didn't taste none too bad!

The next night, we decided we needed eggs for that cornbread. That was more of a problem, cause where there were eggs, there were chickens, and chickens weren't the quietest. We loaded our pockets with rocks and each had a knife. Splitting into two again, off we went in different directions.

This time we found a farm about five miles from camp with a big old hen house. The place had dogs, though. Roberts surprised me when he threw a rock and hit one right in the head. He hit another, then took out his knife, slicing its neck right through. Guess we would have dog for breakfast if nothing else.

We advanced on the henhouse fast. We had to get in and out before squawking brought out farmers with guns, if there were farmers at all. More likely, women took care of these hens. Women could be fiercer with a shotgun than any man.

Roberts moved right through, severing heads left and right while I plucked eggs from nests. Sure enough, seven hens and a mess of eggs later, we got out of there at the sound of a shotgun. One of the others had the dog, and we ran for our lives, but they got on mules and tried to get us. We hauled ass cross-country and met up with the rest who had some luck too.

Next morning, we had us some nice pancakes and fried eggs—yes we did—with a little bit of meat on the side which I didn't take to. Didn't look like no chicken to me.

That night we had ourselves a chicken wing or two, but now had the attention of the rest of the company. We tried taking our food off away from the others, but you can't hide the smell of chicken frying in a pan—no sirree Bob—and we were called up to headquarters for a good talking-to.

How he knew who did it, I don't know, but he had every single one of us standing there. We stood at attention while the commander walked around us.

"Men," he said, "I hear you're not satisfied with the rations we give you."

Nobody said nothing.

"I'll tell you once, and I won't say it again." Pacing up and down in front of the row of ten, he looked each of us sternly in the eye. "If I ever hear of any of you leaving your quarters for any reason other than an order you've received from a higher-up, I'll have you court-martialed. Do you understand?"

"Yes, sir!" we answered in unison.

"I've also received reports of men sneaking out at night, coming back just before dawn. You wouldn't know anything about that, would you?"

"No, sir!"

"I've had complaints from all over the county of animals and grain being stolen. You wouldn't know about that now, would you, boys?"

"No, sir!"

"We're here to protect the citizens in these parts, not steal from them. Well, just to make sure, I'm giving each of you night-watch duty. We wouldn't want anyone sneaking out of here now, would we?"

"No, sir!"

"Report to your sergeants. They'll give you your duty times. That's all."

"Yes, sir!"

"Dis-missed."

We turned as one and marched out the door. Didn't look at one another all the way back to camp.

We were also put on latrine duty. No one ever charged us outright with the crimes, but they knew, and that ended our evening sojourns—for a while.

Things weren't good in camp, though. More troops marched out every day to other places that needed help. Some went south, some west. We stayed put. Don't ask me why. Our regiment wasn't the first created, but we weren't the last either. Didn't seem like they had us doing nothing important, and that got to us.

Roberts complained all the time. Got so I was sorry we was tent-mates. I had other friends now but I wasn't 'bout to tell him I wanted out.

Finally, one day I had it and had to say so. We dug side by side, covering up old latrines.

"Worst goddamn job in the army, and look who's doing it," he said.

I couldn't argue, but all the cussing and fussing was getting on my nerves.

"Never get to do nothing that means something," he continued. "Always low man on the totem pole."

I already pointed out that somebody had to do it, that it took muscle, and that it was important work.

"Trash work, that's what it is," he complained. "Treat us worse than poor white trash."

I stopped, stuck my shovel in the ground, and leaned up against it. "You know, Roberts," I said.

He kept working.

"I'm sick and tired of hearing you bitch and complain all day and all night. Ain't no better for nobody else doing this than it is for you. But you're the only one that does nothing but complain."

He stopped and dug his shovel in next to mine and looked down at me. "Listen here, you little shit," he said. "There's more to living than this. I won't dig latrines for the rest of my life. The way it looks, that's all they think we's good for. You see anybody anywhere doing anything worthwhile? They got us doing the worst of the worst cause the white man won't."

"Everybody knows that. You ain't saying nothing new. Just makes it worse to hear you complain all the time." I picked up my shovel. "Quit moaning and groaning, man. Makes it harder for everybody."

"Everybody better hear it," he said louder now, "cause it ain't right. You don't wanna hear it cause you don't wanna think it. But it's the God's truth I'm telling you." Now he was shouting. "We's better than this and you know it." He shook his head, quieting hisself down. "Look at you. You can read and write and what they got you doing?"

I sighed. Wasn't no getting round the truth of what he said, but putting up with the work on top of his bitching was more than I could handle. I dug in with my shovel. "You ain't making it easier."

"You got that right." He picked up his. "And I don't mean to, neither."

Couple months of night duty and digging latrines by day was about all Roberts could take. Add his griping, and it was all I could do to get up in the morning. Down the way, others sang while they worked, trying to make it a brighter day.

That just put old Roberts in a worse mood. "Dumb shits play right in the hands of them whites. This ain't no free town. You know it and so do I. There'll be slaves here even after this war, no matter who wins." He worked faster as he got madder. "They's so happy working for their nice white bosses. Think they got it easy." He shoveled away, working up a head of steam. "Ain't no way we got it easy here and never will. Look how they feed us." Dug like he was going right to China. "Every week less and less. You'd think they's running out of rations."

It was true. They had thinned our rations till we began to look and feel like we were in a prison camp rather than This Man's Army.

"We got no say, Jeb, no say at all in what happens to us, whether we be in this-here regiment or out of it. Somehow we always work for the white man. That's gotta stop. There's gotta be a way."

So went his rant, every day the same, till the day Jake—another digger—came down our way.

"Listen," he whispered.

I thought he'd get on Roberts like the rest for putting them at risk with his raving, but that wasn't the case.

"I heard tell of a group leaving to go north."

Roberts kept digging. "I'm listening," he said real low.

"They's a community of people of color near some city where everybody works for everybody else, and nobody works for no white man."

"That right?" Roberts asked, still digging.

Jake dug on Roberts's other side now. "Even have their own stores and businesses. Do a lot of bartering—trading—you know."

"How far up?"

"Near Cleveland."

I didn't know Cleveland, but Malek on my other side spoke up. "Cleveland! That's clear up by Pennsylvania."

"Farther from here the better," said Roberts as he dug. "When?"

"We collecting things now. Plan to leave in three nights."

"Count me in," said Roberts.

"Y'all's nuts," said Malek.

Jake walked over and grabbed Malek by the shirt. "You leak this before or after we go, and you're dead. Hear?"

"Hey, hey!" shouted the sergeant behind us. There had been more and more fights lately. The troops weren't happy. No sir. "Break it up!"

Malek shrugged Jake off. "I didn't hear nothing," he said.

"Back to your station," the sergeant ordered Jake.

"Station," grunted Roberts. "Like it was some post."

The sergeant came up behind him. "What'd you say, boy?"

Roberts kept working. "Better go back to his station's what I said."

The sergeant watched us, then left.

Nobody said nothing for a long time. Mealtime came, and off I went to think. Sure, it was bad here. And it wasn't gonna get better, the way it looked. We didn't hear much about which way the War was going. Every morning at reveille, our commander told us what he thought we needed to know for the day. Sometimes we got a pep talk with the results of the latest Union victory. New recruits coming over the river every night told of Rebs getting routed or the other way around, but you never got a feel for the whole of what was really going on.

Turns out, even though Cincinnati was part of the Union, it did have its own way of thinking about slaves. Not every Union state was for abolition, and not every city in every abolitionist state was for it. Cincinnati definitely was not. If you got caught in Cincinnati, you got sent back, though laws were changing.

If you were in the military though, you were safe cause you were needed. Not that you were defending the North, but you helped those that did defend it. Like the good wife standing behind her husband, supporting him, we good coloreds were in the background. But we were there, no two ways about that. We were there.

I sat, my back against a tree, with decisions to make. If I went with Roberts and the group, we'd be back to running and hiding. Was that worse than this? If we ran, we might be captured. What then? Laws had changed. If we got farther north, we couldn't be sent back to our owners no more. If we got caught, they'd probably send us to prison—no worse than now. Of course, getting shot was most likely, if you thought about it.

Was the cost of giving up life worth the chance to be totally free? Was life worth living if this was what it would be like? Then again, life couldn't stay this way. Maybe we'd go off like those colored troops who left for battlefields Out West. Besides, the War couldn't go on forever, could it? Things were bound to change.

But what would I do without Roberts?

"What you thinking so hard about?" The only true friend I had sat down beside me. Not that the others weren't friendly, but I knew that he kept some from making fun of me. I owed him for that. Hell, I owed him a lot.

"I'm thinking about when we're leaving, that's what," I said, like there wasn't no question about it.

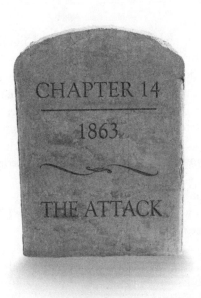

CHAPTER 14

1863

THE ATTACK

What you do—or don't do—matters.
—J. Johnson

A new moon blessed us with a dark night. We waited till Willard gave the signal. A small stone hit our tent as he walked by to the latrine. We crawled out. Nelson, on guard duty that night, followed the rest of us. We sortied together same as before—off the road, around the bend, behind a big rock—ten of us, big men save for me.

Stars twinkled, showing the way. We hiked as the crow flies, moving fast as we could. Knew what would happen when we weren't in our places at reveille. They'd break out a posse on horseback with hounds tracking us like they did every time there was a break, then give up and go back if we got far enough ahead. It was almost routine. One or two deserted every day, but never ten at once. They didn't pursue the others like they could. Too much else to do, just to keep an eye on everything and keep the ranks simmered down.

You can't keep good fighting men doing slave work, just like you can't treat an adult like a child. You just don't do that.

We let our hot heads lead us, instead of figuring out a plan. Once we got clear of the danger of being chased—well, that was as far ahead as anybody thought out. We knew we wanted to get to one of them places where the coloreds did for themselves and not the white man—or any town that wasn't proslavery.

After not being caught the first couple of nights, we got traveling by day since we was free, every now and then stopping for water at a drinking pump for coloreds in some little podunk town along the road.

"Any communities round here where coloreds work for coloreds?" we'd ask when we seen one of our kind. "Like having their own shops and stores?"

They'd look around, their eyes wide like they never heard tell of no such thing and were afraid to be talking such. Which told us we were way too far south yet.

The other problem? Ten coloreds roaming the road together didn't look good. People gave us plenty of space as we moved through town. Some whites even went hiding when they seen us a-coming. Problem was, the coloreds were afraid too. Just wasn't right, people being so afraid of us.

"How come our own look at us like that?" I asked as a few blacks veered off the road before we got to them. Up till that fifth day, we didn't understand it.

Now I gots to tell you, we all stowed rations before leaving camp. Even though the food wasn't enough in the first place, we'd need it on the road even more. At first, everybody had biscuits and all, but it sure wasn't enough when we were on the move. Hell, most of us ate up all we had the first day or so.

Foraging for food was pretty easy at first cause it was harvest time. We found plenty in the fields. But we needed meat too. That meant going into smokehouses again, getting closer to homes. At night when we searched for food, we circled around a farm real good, closing in real slow to make sure no dogs would give us away.

In towns, people were a-scared of us, so we broke up in twos and threes and begged at the backs of inns, eating places, and boardinghouses. One colored lady came to the back step of a big old home and gave us some real good pea soup right there in the kitchen. Sent us off the next morning with cornbread and cooked sausages for the whole group. Don't know how they had so much at that home, but we were mighty grateful. Yes, we were. We did okay those first few days—found what we needed without getting caught.

As we went farther north though, it got harder to get food cause we began to stay away from towns. We really didn't want to cause more distrust than we already had, looking like a pack of hungry wolves, though we found out fast that there truly is strength in numbers.

We weren't the only ones prowling around looking for eats. Other bands of deserters and wanderers circled away when they seen how many we had when we were together, and we stayed clear of them. Didn't want no trouble. Just wanted to get someplace where we could settle down and earn a living. Forget fighting the War. We done that already.

The fact that others like us were out and about making trouble made it harder for us to get what we needed. Once again, hunger became the enemy. Soon we found ourselves behaving no better than they did. Survival was the name of the game and we had to eat. So we broke into two groups like we used to, and set out to get some vittles.

One night about three weeks into our journey, we came upon a right nice looking farm with a few outbuildings kept up real good. It was just past dark and the house was all lit up inside.

Roberts, being the biggest, always gave the orders and I stuck by him.

"You two," he said, gesturing to Nelson and Hudson, "go round and see what's in them sheds."

They took off quiet-like, bent low.

"Georgie, take your group around the barn. See what's there." A group of five started for the small white barn behind the house.

Roberts didn't give orders to me or Reuben or Washington, the only ones left. He just skirted round the left of the house and we followed. Stooping low, we could see inside. Looked all warm and cozy, it sure did. Around back, a lady with light hair moved about in her kitchen. A pretty thing, she was. We moved on, looking for cellar doors leading into the ground.

"No root cellar?" whispered Washington.

"Shush!" whispered Roberts.

We heard people coming towards us from the other side of the house and met up with the rest of the group, everybody empty-handed.

"Well if that don't beat all," said Roberts, when we regrouped out of hearing range. "They must have it all stockpiled inside. We're not the first to come scrounging around." He sat back on his haunches while we huddled.

The smell of frying chicken wafted by. All ten faces turned to the house.

"That's more than I can stand," said Morrison.

We hadn't ever raided a house with people in it. But we were so damned hungry. We had to eat.

"Washington, you and Nelson go round front and knock on the door, hats in your hands, real nice-like. While you talk with the lady, we'll go in the back way and get what we can. Everybody meet after we're done back at the last orchard we passed just before this-here farm."

We crept towards the house. Aromas we hadn't smelled in what seemed a lifetime tortured us as we got closer. Peeking just above the kitchen windowsills, we seen her go through an open door into the dining room and set down with three pretty little children. They bowed their heads in grace.

The mama jumped up to get the front door.

"Now!" whispered Roberts.

He tried the kitchen door but it was locked, then he pushed against it quiet-like, but it didn't budge. Cursing, he threw his shoulder into it with all his might, breaking down the door and surprising everybody inside and out. None of us were ready for that, but we ran right behind him into a house filled with the highest-pitched screaming you ever did hear.

We had to get in and out fast, and filled our pockets with anything edible from the cupboards and counters. Reuben grabbed some empty flour bags hanging from a hook next to the door and charged into the dining room.

The little lady had us fooled. There she stood, a shotgun pointing from her hip at Ned and Hudson who had pushed the door open from the front when we came in the back. They stood with their hands on their heads, and we froze.

The little blondies kept screaming and ran to be beside their mother.

"Get under the table," she yelled at them. They did as they were told.

She looked at Roberts and us behind him. "Move another inch and I'll blow their heads off."

None of us doubted she would do just that.

"Look, lady," said Roberts. "We don't mean to scare you. We's just hungry."

"I ain't got nothing to give you," she said. "Hardly got enough for my own. Now, git outta my house this instant or they're goners." She held that gun, a-swaying a little to and fro but targeted on the two of them just the same. At that range, she'd get one or the other first time around. No doubt about it.

The little ones huddled under the table. I couldn't see nothing but their shoes, but I heard their sobs.

This just wasn't right.

Roberts must have felt the same way, cause he spoke up. "Lady, we's gonna back outta here real easy now so you can go back to your table."

She saw our bulging pockets and made her first mistake, turning the gun slightly our way. "Take everything outta . . ."

When she hesitated, the tide turned.

". . . outta your pockets . . . , you ruthless no-good—"

Before she finished, Nelson was on her and grabbed the gun.

"No!" she screamed, but Washington jumped into the fray. Nelson turned the gun on her.

The rest of us moved around the table. Washington dragged her into the front hallway as she fought and scratched him a good one.

"Ouch! Goddammit!" shouted Washington, touching his cheek where she got him. His hand came away bloody. He looked back at her, a new and ugly light in his eye. "Why you little . . ."

Before you could blink, he ripped her bodice down and shoved her to the floor. Nelson, nervous and wavering now, kept the gun on her.

Roberts grabbed more empty flour sacks hanging in the kitchen. "Get those kids outta here," he said, throwing the sacks to Hudson. "Tie them up in these."

Hudson and Morrison dove under from opposite sides of the table, grabbing for the children. Hudson came out with two, screaming and kicking. Morrison had the third gagged with a cloth napkin, the sack over the child's head, and tied to a kitchen chair in no time. Reuben ran around, kicking over chairs to get at the two tussling with Hudson. All four of them fell over together—Hudson, Reuben, and the two kids—when the little one's dress flew up.

A group intake of breath. Holding her down, Morrison stuffed her mouth with a napkin but didn't do nothing about that dress as muffled screams and deep guttural grunts of another nature echoed from the front parlor.

My stomach turned. I couldn't do this. I couldn't watch. I couldn't listen to it. Nauseous, I grabbed the table for balance, then turned and pushed my way past the others, making for the out-of-doors. Running through the kitchen, I emptied my pockets of everything and stumbled outside and down the steps, retching. Gasping for air, I ran and ran and finally stopped far from the house and vomited. There wasn't nothing in me to vomit, yet vomit I did. I fell to the ground, pulled my knees to my chin and rocked, crying like a baby while the horrors in that house continued.

A shot rang out.

I sat up and looked towards the house. Men charged out the door, heading my way. I jumped up and hobbled away, trying to run with them. Bent over and retching still, my stomach cramped again, my foot giving extra problems.

Hudson ran by, shouting, "Roberts done killed Morrison," and kept going. Two more rushed by, then came Roberts, hauling ass.

"Find a place to hide," he yelled back at me.

Suddenly, it was just me in that field. The house, a ways back and still lit up, stood with its back door yawning wide open to the night, cozy no more. Those children all tied up. That one little girl. And their mama. A dead man in the house. What must they be doing right now?

Should I go back?

Hogwash. If I went back, I'd end up in jail.

There was nothing I could do for them. Nothing.

I passed out.

CHAPTER 15

1863

THE WINDOW

I seen all this play out over and over in my mind's eye.
—J. Johnson

A rooster crowed before daybreak. My stomach in knots, I tried to sit up but could raise nothing but my head. I wasn't in the field. And I wasn't outside.

Memories of the night crept in, and I began to sweat and heave all over again. I couldn't move my hands or feet. Why, I couldn't move at all! What held me down? I couldn't even open my eyes.

I must be dreaming, I thought, and everything went black.

Again, the cock crowed. *That* wasn't no dream. I tried to open my eyes, but couldn't. *What the hell?* I tried to move my fingers and toes. Nothing worked.

Whispers and footsteps. A woman's voice. "I'll check and let you know."

Someone stopped next to the bed. A light hand took my wrist, held it a moment, and set it down, felt my forehead, then mopped it with a cool cloth. Sure felt good. Sounds of scratching, like writing. The footsteps faded.

I fell back into my stupor.

Loud voices out the window brought me to myself again, and I sure didn't like it. My stomach hurt something awful. My head wasn't much better. I opened my eyes to a flowery room with pretty little curtains. A nun fussing about the bed looked up to see me watching her. Where the hell was I?

"Oh, hello!" she said.

If she knew I could talk, she might ask questions—too many questions.

"You were in pretty bad shape when they found you out in that field."

I wanted to ask, *Who? Who found me?*

"Most fortunate they gave that field over to the parish for upkeep or we might not have found you." She came around the side of the bed and sat down.

Leave me alone, lady.

"Why," she rambled on, "we were out turning over the old crop for winter when Sister Marietta cried out and there you were! You must have been there all night, from the looks of things," she said, a question now in her voice.

She could see I wasn't gonna say a thing. "Well!" She stood, smiling down on me. "I'm glad to see you're with us again. The sisters will be so happy to know you're awake." Stopping at the door, she said, "I expect you want something to eat. I'll ask Sister Marguerite to warm up a little supper for you."

Brisk footsteps faded down the hallway leaving me to my thoughts, and they weren't pretty. What had we done? Going into that house, knowing people were in there, was insane. I knew it, Roberts knew it for sure, and them others—were they fools or what? Even if it was our business to find food, it wasn't our business to go in a house, much less one with people in it. We were asking for trouble. That plan to distract them with a beggar's call would be fool's luck if it worked. And look what happened. That mother being hurt and then that little . . .

The thought of Morrison and that child. I was sure glad Roberts stopped it, even if it meant killing Morrison. But that made Roberts a killer. And me—what did they call it when you

helped out? An "accomplish" or something like that. I helped
out on the break-in. Sure I did. But I ran when I seen what was
coming and didn't have nothing to do with the rest of it.

Or did I? Could I have stopped it? I could have fought
Morrison off that little girl. Maybe the others would have
helped. But maybe they wanted what Morrison was getting too.
A man of honor would at least say something to bring them to
their senses before it all got out of hand. But I hadn't.

How did we get to the place where we let such a thing happen? I never thought it in me to allow something like that. But
then, I always let others make the decisions. It wasn't the easy
way out—in fact, it made for hard living—but it kept me from
facing up to sit-yations that were out of my control anyway.

Roberts and Morrison and Hudson and Nelson and all the
others—even me—we were angry. People like this little family—look what they had, and we had none. But there was nothing I could do about it, so I left it be. So it grew and festered
and became something terrible. No sir, I could not justify what
we done. I didn't touch them, but I was part of it just the same
cause I didn't stop it.

When people don't say nothing, in a way they're saying
"yes," cause they let it happen. They're sure as hell not saying
"no." Like me. I stood there, and when it got too much, instead
of saying something that might make more trouble, I turned
and left, dropping my stolen meat on the way.

Who wanted to eat? Who was hungry? Who could have an
appetite? Not me. Not after that.

Lying in that bed, I still didn't.

Wasn't long before another sister glided through the door.
"I hear you're awake and ready to eat," she said with a smile.
"Now, sit up." She set the tray on a side table, on it a steaming
bowl of soup, biscuits, a glass of milk, even a hard-cooked egg.

I took one look and wanted to puke. Here I broke into a
house for food. Now I couldn't look at it. I turned away.

"Oh, come now," she said, fluffing my pillow to get me to
sit up, but I wouldn't. "You must eat or you'll lose your
strength."

She had a point there. I didn't want to be no weakling. I turned back to face the tray, but my stomach turned again. I must have looked green.

"Oh, dear. You must be sicker than Sister thought."

I didn't wake again till the next day when the first sister-nurse came in, opening the curtains like she thought I'd slept enough. "Good morning!"

Why were they always so cheery?

"And a bright day it is too. Just look at it!" She stood a moment, gazing at the sunny fall day.

I looked out the window. Nothing but trouble out there.

Wait. They kept slaves on the run from The Law in sanctuaries. Was I in a sanctuary now? Would they turn me over to the authorities if they thought I might be part of the band that raided that house? Surely The Law must be looking for us. Whether this was a hospital or just where the nuns lived, it was part of the church, right? To protect me, would the sisters need to know I was innocent? Did I have to ask them to keep me safe from The Law, or would they just do it?

Was I really innocent?

I couldn't get through these thoughts fast enough.

She was at my side. "Well! You look much better this morning."

Why don't she say nothing about what happened? We must be near that field. . . .

"Maybe you'd like to eat today?"

She didn't seem to be hiding nothing, like she knew what happened or that they were looking for a group of black men and one of them had a twisted foot. Maybe she didn't know.

"Can you hear me, sir?"

I had to decide. Was it better to go on playing dumb and mute?

If they weren't looking for nobody, I didn't have to. I turned to her and drawled, "What's that?"

"Oh, hallelujah!" she cried, beside herself with joy. "Sir, you had us so worried."

I tried to look innocent. "I did?" Nobody ever called me "sir" before.

"We were afraid you'd lost all sense of things."

Maybe I *should* have kept my mouth shut and played dumb. No. I'd be easy to identify whether I talked or not. Wait. They never seen me walk yet. They didn't know about my . . . sure they did. Just look at it and you knew.

"I'll go tell Sister Edwina to fix you some toast," she said, bustling out the door.

Toast didn't sound no better this morning than soup did last night, but I didn't say nothing. I had some thinking to do.

The news of our raid on that poor family should have been all over the place by now. Why hadn't the sisters told the authorities I was here? Cause I was a runaway, and they were keeping me safe?

I looked out the window across the fields to a farmhouse. My eyes widened. Sitting up, I squinted to make sure I was right.

In walked Sister Marguerite.

I jumped.

"Oh!" she laughed. "Didn't mean to startle you." She brung another tray to the bedside table. This time it was toast and honey and a little oatmeal. Was that brown sugar on it? Real brown sugar?

I leaned closer to have a better look.

"Looks like you have an appetite today. Now, let's sit up and see if you can't take some nourishment."

Oh my, it smelled good. As I scooted back to sit up, she fluffed the pillows behind my back. But the window across from the bed showed a picture I didn't want to see. I squeezed my eyes shut as if against the sun.

"Could—could you shut that curtain? The sun . . ."

She placed the tray on my lap. "Oh! Of course, dear. Does it hurt your eyes?"

"Yes . . . yes, it does," I said, shading them so I couldn't see.

Pulling the drapes, she darkened the room, but inside my head that outside picture would not go away. I looked down at the meal that a minute ago looked so good, but I couldn't eat cause I couldn't stomach what I done.

"Oh, dear," she said, reading my look. "I'm afraid that sunlight took away your appetite."

I nodded, feeling worse.

She took the tray. "Just lie back now."

I slid under the covers and rolled over to go back to sleep. Except I couldn't. Every time I closed my eyes I seen that house. I'd know that farm any time of day, any time of year, in any kind of weather. Wasn't no way I could forget that farm and that house and that family and what we done to them.

I couldn't understand, with that farm so close, why the people at this-here church house didn't know what happened. Unless . . .

The mama. That was it! She wouldn't want nobody to know. She and her little girl would be sullied for life. She wouldn't want her husband to know either. And if he was dead from the War, something like this would ruin her. Same for the little girl.

But what about Morrison? If he was shot and left there to die, she'd have to get the authorities. Or not. What if she took care of it herself and she and them kids was the only ones alive—except for us what did it—to know what happened that night? What if she . . .

Oh God Almighty. That poor lady. She dragged him out all by herself and buried him! I could just see her digging that grave. What a lot of work for a poor little thing like that. Specially after what happened. And those beautiful babies—the one all battered, the others tied up. Did they go to school the next day like nothing happened and never told nobody about it?

Jesus Christ Almighty, I prayed, *come down and help that family. Jesus! Oh Jesus God.*

I cried myself to sleep.

Later that day, I thought and thought, and knew I had to get out. To do that, I had to be strong. To be that, I had to eat.

Funny thing about starvation. Worse it gets, the less you want to eat. After a few weeks with Roberts and the group, I just stopped wanting. Ever after that, when I had a problem in my head I couldn't handle, the first thing to kick in was lack of appetite. Took it right away. First sign of trouble, forget eating.

So now, this bag of skin and bones had to make hisself eat. Oh, and weren't those nuns happy when the tide turned and I accepted their offerings.

"Oh, Mr. Johnson!" praised Sister Edwina later that afternoon when I told her my name and she found I ate up all the soup she left me. "You did eat, didn't you!" She picked up the tray and paused. "Would you like more, Mr. Johnson?"

"Ma'am," says I, rubbing my tummy in circles, "I'm plum satisfied. But I wish you'd just call me by my first name." I was getting to like them nuns.

"Surely, Mr. Johnson, if that's what you prefer." She stood, waiting.

"Oh, it's Jeb, ma'am," I said. "Jeb Johnson." I was through confusing people with the *s* on my other name. Told that story once too often. Besides, it was time I had my own name and not be known by nobody else's.

I knew they might catch me if I told them that name. I don't know why I did it. Nobody but the bandits and the army knew me as Jeb Johnson. Course that was bad enough.

"All right, Jeb," she said, clearing the tray to the hallway. She came back in to pull the curtains.

"Oh please, ma'am," I said. "Please don't open them."

"But Mr. Johnson—Jeb," she corrected herself, "the sunlight's clear over to the other side now. It won't bother you." She started to pull them back.

"Please," I said, covering my eyes.

She closed them back up. "You'll see it differently in the morning."

I had to get out of there. The sooner, the better.

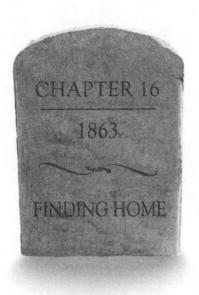

CHAPTER 16

1863

FINDING HOME

Nothing's small when you look at it close enough—
everything points to something bigger.
—J. Johnson

"Well, Jeb," said Sister Edwina as she opened all the curtains but one. "You've been eating very well these last few days."

"Yes, ma'am, I'm feeling real good, thanks to you sisters," I said, hoping she thought I felt better than I really did, so I could leave.

"You know, Jeb, the only health problem we figure you had is severe malnutrition."

Surprise, surprise.

"Someday soon, the light from that window won't hurt your eyes so. Then we'll know you're ready for the outdoors."

"Oh, ma'am. It ain't the light." How could I keep from seeing that house again? "It . . . that house reminds me of back home, is all."

"Really," she said, giving me a strange look. Opening the curtain a crack, she peeked through. "I'd think the architecture down in Arkansas would be different."

"Alabama. Yes, ma'am. But those outbuildings . . ."

"I see."

"I'm better, ain't I?"

She left the room without another word. Maybe she knew what happened in that house after all. But they kept the curtains closed and didn't mention it again.

One morning Sister Edwina carried in a pile of clothes, plopped them on the end of the bed and said, "Get dressed."

I looked around for my own clothes, but she shook her head. "Burned them."

Surprised, I sat up. "But . . ."

"Not fit for a human being."

"But my spectacles . . ."

"Oh! I forgot." Reaching into her pocket, she pulled them out, all nice and clean.

I put them on and could see again. I looked over what she brung: three pair of good sturdy overalls, undergarments, a couple of shirts, shoes and socks like I never worn. It was a good-sized stack, more than enough for just little old me.

"Thank you, ma'am," I said, "but I don't think I can carry all this."

She laughed. "See what fits, Jeb. The rest stays here."

All of them looked good. "I ain't never worried about size before, ma'am." I got a little nervous. "I'm not quite sure what you mean."

"Here," she said, handing me a shirt. "I'll help you. Put that on." She laughed again at the look I gave her. "Oh, don't worry. I bathed you when you were delirious, Mr. Johnson. There's no part of you I haven't seen."

I do believe I blushed.

"All right," she said, giving in with a smile. "I'll turn my back."

She got me all suited up and when I left the parish house or nunnery or whatever-you-call-it later that week, I had me a fine big old hat on my head, a pack full of clothes and dried food on my back, water in my canteen, a scratched-out map, and a couple of coins in my pocket. You can't beat that. No sir.

Turns out they were part of the Underground Railroad. Yes indeedy. The Good Lord must have heard my prayer out there in the field, cause He up and landed me in that fine place with those fine people who helped me get better, then sent me off well fed and well dressed. Don't get no better.

I left under cover of the stars. And you can bet I didn't go towards that house across the field. In fact, the first night I went due north to a place just ten miles away. They started me out slow, and wise that was, cause besides being weak, winter was close by and it was right cold.

By the time I got to that first place, I was plum tuckered. Found me a pallet all made up and ready in a back barn, a lantern by its side with fresh biscuits, honey, an apple, and some milk—like they expected me. I don't know how those nuns done it, but I never seen such storybook gallantry as I did in them.

"Anti-abolitionists abound all the way up, even past Michigan into Canada," the nuns warned. They worked out the routes runaways took, depending on where people wanted to go, which was decided pretty much by the sit-yation in different parts of these so-called "United" States. You went where the conditions would be best for you. They knew I wanted Cleveland, though, and don't you know that's exactly where this map would take me!

In the future, I would meet others like me at some stops. Then there'd be places like this first one where nobody said hello or goodbye. But it was nice and ready and I felt welcomed, yes I did. "Jeb" Jacobs Johnson was welcome here. Praise the Lord.

Thinking back, except for my mama and the nuns and this place, I don't think I ever felt welcomed. Nobody ever said nothing like, "Welcome to my place." That word "welcome" is powerful.

Some white folk were awful good to me on my journey. Then again, their job was to protect me from the whites that weren't so good. It was that way with people of any race— some were kind and some not. Them that weren't didn't know that every heart and every soul comes from the same place. We're all the same, before life and after. I'll get into that "after" part later, when the time comes. Oh yes I will.

The farther north I got, the slower I traveled. Winter made it hard to get from one place to the next. I'd work a day here or there to buy food. Later, when I found a safe place, I'd stay a week or two. Then a month or two. Each stop got a little more comfortable. Fact was, I was tired of moving, moving, moving. The idea of staying, instead of leaving, grew on me till I just couldn't get up and leave no more. Besides, the War finally ended and I didn't need to hide.

So here I came into this place bigger than any city I been to—mile after mile after mile of people, mostly whites. The blacks worked the lowest jobs, just like always, and had to walk miles to and from them.

Where's the community? I asked myself. I couldn't find it.

One day, I followed a colored lady home. She walked blocks and blocks, then rode a flatbed towards the center of town. Cost a penny to ride, but I got on and paid too.

When she got off, I got off and, lo and behold, wasn't I surrounded by people of color just like me! Some even talked like me. I was just so happy to walk up and down the streets saying hello to this person and that, I didn't care that I hadn't had supper or if my shoes had holes in them, cause I was home. Yes, I was. Didn't go no farther. Didn't have to. I found my people.

Got a place to stay with other gentlemen in a home cared for by the Central AME (African Methodist Episcopalian—if that don't mix you up) Church next door. This church was the core of the whole community. Thing is, the church decided to get the community up on its feet. And we in the home next door? Why, the church felt we could earn our keep by helping.

When they found out I could read and write, that was it for me. I was a schoolteacher and I wasn't teaching no children, no sirree Bob. I taught the men in my house so we could do our own shopping—understand prices and how to count out our money. That was the first thing everybody needed to be able to do.

Next on their list was to read the Bible. You don't think no church is gonna let you go round without knowing its own teachings, do you? That's where your bread and butter came from if you lived in a house furnished by the church, like ours. When they passed that collection plate every Sunday, we ended up giving nearly every penny we earned right back.

Then one Sunday I met me a lady, pretty little thing with a hat tipped just so. Couldn't keep my eyes off her. She noticed me. I know she did, cause she kept looking over her shoulder at me during the service and smiling. Oh yes, that woman smiled right at me. Met my eye and held it.

I walked up to her after church. A couple of matrons had her over to the side. I touched her elbow. She turned around, surprised, then smiled.

Now understand, even with my turned foot, I got to be one of the more distinguished of the lot cause I was a teacher. Didn't mean much outside that little community, but inside, it was everything. I dressed the part and had a nice cane to keep me from bending sideways when I walked down the street. It was all in the way you carried yourself, like you expected others to look on you with respect and dignity. You might say I had an attitude about it. Oh yes indeedy, I was a real ladies' man.

"Hello." Her voice sounded like wind chimes.

"You are just the prettiest thing this place has ever seen," I said.

"Aren't you the charmer."

Strangest thing, it was almost like we were in a space all by ourselves, darkness all around, but full of light right where we stood.

"Ma'am, I got to tell you, I'm the one that's charmed here. You done cast a spell right over me."

"Hi, Jeb." Carlin Lincoln walked by, pulling me back to reality. Took on the president's name when she got free, just like me, except I picked the next one down the list. Carlin and I got into it when I first arrived. Had us a time for a short while, but Carlin wasn't my type—too clingy. Like now—she seen me talking with this new lady and wanted to get in the way. Who needed a woman like that anyway?

"Carlin," I said, tipping my hat without giving my thoughts away.

I turned back to the new lady and offered her my arm. "Ma'am, I'd like to introduce myself. My name is Jeb Johnson and I'm the teacher here."

"Pleased to make your acquaintance, Mr. Johnson," she said with a nod and slight curtsy. "My name is Theresa Williams."

Whoo-ee! Wasn't she the fancy thing. Dressed fancy too. Except for her color, she sure didn't look like she belonged in this crowd.

"Well, Miss Theresa," said I, "may I escort you into the fellowship hall? They've got some mighty fine eats just a-waiting for you and me."

I took her arm and led her through the crowd, claiming her. This woman was mine and no brother would get close now.

We strolled into the hall. Wasn't a fancy church, but it was a good one and they were good people too. I introduced her to some, and we got us food to eat and sat down to talk. I couldn't keep my eyes off her.

CHAPTER 17

1865

FINDING LOVE

I gots to tell you that, when I was telling this story, back a chapter or two ago, my stomach turned, and this author's did too.
—J. Johnson

Saturday rolled around, and I got all dressed up to call on Miss Williams. Had no trouble finding the place—a few blocks down and a few doors over. Turns out she stayed at a ladies' home not unlike my men's home.

I picked her up and we went down to the ice cream shop. Mmm, how I loved to watch her eat her sundae. She was so delicate about it, working her way around the scoop of ice cream, getting the chocolate first, then moving to the top. Made a man think about things he shouldn't on his first time out with a lady.

I called on Miss Williams regularly. We were an item, you could say.

After a few months, though, she got fidgety, then downright fussy. One night, she finally did it.

"I can't see you next week," she said.

"Why?" I asked. "Something wrong? What did I do?"

She sighed. "Jeb, it ain't what you do or don't do." She sat down next to me on a park bench. "I just want to be able to go out with other men too. That's all."

"Ain't I enough for you?"

"Jeb, you're enough for anyone," she said. "I just want to have some fun before I settle down to one man."

"We been having fun all along." I looked at her close. "You talking about a different kind of fun? Cause if that's what you want, I can give you that too."

The woman slapped me across the cheek and stood up. "Jeb Johnson, don't you ever say nothing like that to me again!" She burst into tears and stormed down the street.

Nighttime in the city's not safe for a lady walking alone and, seeing as how she was my responsibility that evening, I ran to catch up. "Theresa, darling," I said, but she kept right on walking. I caught up again and took her elbow. "Honey," I began.

She tried to pull away. "Don't!"

I held onto her and she shook this way and that and finally just covered her face with her hands and started to cry. Not knowing what else to do, I surrounded her with my arms. We made our way back to the bench, and I took a good listen.

"I can't keep this up," she said through tears, then broke down all over again.

"Keep what up?"

"This show I'm putting on. It's nothing but a show."

"What you talking about?"

She quieted, found a hankie and wiped her eyes. "I'm not who you think I am, Jeb."

"I think you're lovely. Can't tell me you're not lovely."

"Jeb, you think I'm good and I'm not."

"Course you're good."

"You have no idea where I come from."

"I don't care about that," I said. "You think any of us come from a good place?"

"But Jeb, you were just a slave. I was . . . I . . ." She burst into tears.

Putting my arm around her, I asked, "You what?" I knew what she was gonna say, and I was right.

"I slept with my owner."

"Course you did. Girl, that happened to every female slave with half your looks. That's a given fact." The thought had come to me from time to time. No woman who looked like her was gonna get out of being a slave without first belonging to her owner in a womanly way.

"For years, Jeb. Since I was little."

"So? That make you bad?"

She was quiet, then took a big breath and said, "I loved him."

That put a different light on things.

"You loved him? You loved your owner?"

She nodded, wiping her tears away again. "When he went to fight, I waited, but he never came home. When the letter came saying he was dead, my life there was over. Everybody hated me. I left after that."

Took a few minutes for me to cogitate on that one. "I can see how that could happen." And I could.

"But there's more."

More?

"We . . . we had children."

Silence. Then, "How many?"

"Just two," she said and smiled. "Harry, he's my youngest, is four now. And Lily—she was the apple of her daddy's eye—she'd be eight." Her eyes got glassy. "When he . . . died, the Mrs. . . . she had children of their own. She felt threatened by my babies, I think, cause he loved them so. So when we knew he was gone for good—it just about killed me to hear about his dying—she . . . she . . ." Tears welled up and she jerked from trying to keep the sob in her chest from coming up.

I waited, my arm still round her shoulder, watching her.

"She sold my babies." Now the tears flowed. I took her in my arms and she cried on my chest a long, long time. "I don't know who she sold them to," she said between sobs. "I don't know where they are. My babies!" she wailed.

Dear God.

After a while, she quieted down. "That's when I left."

This woman couldn't have no daughter eight years of age. "Theresa, a man don't usually ask this of a lady, but how old are you?"

"That's another thing," she said and smiled. "I'm old—twenty-four."

"So? You had the first child when you was sixteen. Lots of women have babies even younger."

"But twenty-four—that's an old maid." She cried all over again.

I rocked her. "There, there, there," I said. "It's gonna be all right." I could handle this. Any owner would be crazy not to sleep with her. I could live with this. I could. So she was a lot older than me. So what? I could take care of her. I would.

"Jeb," she asked.

"Yes, darling?" I was feeling mighty loving right then.

"Mind if I ask how old you are?"

Oh now, wasn't this just the thing. If I told her I was seventeen, that would end it right there. *Oh hell*, I thought. "Old enough," I said, "to take care of you."

"But I want to know . . . how old?"

There weren't no records of my birth except back on that plantation and I doubted records lasted past the War, so I told a little fib.

This is when it really began.

"I'm twenty," said I, looking her straight in the eye. They say liars can't do that, but I did it real fine. Looking at something I wanted more than anything made it easy—too easy.

"Oh," she said, troubled.

Didn't she think twenty was enough?

Nobody at the men's house wanted to insult us so they didn't ask your age or date of birth. Course, when I got baptized—and that was coming up, me being a teacher through the church and all—I'd have to choose a real number. I'd tell them something.

"Or let me think," I said. "Maybe twenty-one. I'm not sure. They didn't keep count at the plantation. Never really knew when my birthday was." Which wasn't true. Knew exactly when it was cause Mama kept track.

"I guess you're old enough for an old maid like me."

"Oh, honey, you're anything but an old lady," I said, getting the conversation off of me and back to her again. I pulled her into my arms. We got closer than ever after that.

One day, I sat by the woodstove in the fellowship hall with a circle of men learning them to read. They weren't real far along. Had their alphabet and numbers down but couldn't put much meaning to the sounds that went with the letters, so I helped them match the two.

"Now, this-here letter, what's that?" I asked.

I had me a more advanced class that worked on sentences and puncty-ation and such, much as I knew anyway, but this class had a long way to go before they'd catch up to the others.

"That'd be *M*," said Jeremiah, an old honky-tonk player from down in Georgia. He never was a slave, just wanted to get out before they burned the place down.

"That's right. Letters don't mean nothing 'less you know what sound they stand for, understand?"

The men nodded a little, like maybe they didn't.

"So this-here *M* sounds like this: 'Mm-mm-mm,'" I said.

Johnny G, youngest in the group, spoke up. "I never heard no word with a long sound like that," he objected. "But I did hear of 'Mm-mm-mm good!'"

Everybody laughed. "That's right, brother!"

"Right, Johnny G," I said. "You put a whole lot of *M*s together and you get that long sound. But when you have a short *em* sound, then it's just one 'mm.'"

Their faces went blank.

"Like the *M* in the word 'man.'"

"There's a *M* in 'man'?" asked Jeremiah.

Johnny G turned to him. "Think about it," he said. "M-man. It's so simple."

"Huh," said old Jeremiah. "M-man. Sure. I get that. But that's just the front of it. What about the rest of it?"

"The end of 'man'?" I said, then turned it back to them. They had to be able to figure this for themselves. "What is that sound?"

"Sound on the end of 'man'?" asked Petey Floyd Morrissey, a young buck with a family coming out of the Carolinas to meet him here any day now. Itchy to see his woman, he worried about where he was gonna put them all and still keep them together. "Well, it would be . . ."

Right then, Pastor Amos came in with a couple of older matrons. Thing is, these women were white. They looked all excited and serious at the same time. We stood for them.

I shook his hand. "Morning, Pastor."

"Morning," he said, shaking hands all around. "Morning. How are ya? Morning to you," till he was done with the bunch of us.

"Gentlemen," he said, "I have something mighty special to share with you this morning, something we in the ecumenical community knew might happen, but didn't really believe it actually could."

Changes happened every day round here. Some for the better, some for the worse. This sounded like it could be good.

"These fine ladies have come to tell me that we're gonna get a *real* school right here in the community. Not just for children, for everybody, so you can all learn to read and write and do numbers."

Everybody brightened but me.

"We're gonna have us an educated teacher too," he said, proud of this new success.

When I told Theresa at the ice cream shop later that week, she didn't like the change either. "You mean you ain't no teacher no more?" she asked, plain disappointed. "What you gonna do?"

"I don't know. Everybody's in the same boat, looking for jobs. I ain't no different than none of the others except for my foot, and that just makes it worse. Nobody looking for fit men is gonna hire me." I thought as I talked. "That leaves office work."

"Can you do that?" she asked, like maybe I couldn't do nothing.

"Theresa, I worked for a bookkeeper. I can do it." Didn't she believe in me?

"Yeah, but you wasn't *the* bookkeeper. You just helped." She twirled her spoon in her ice cream, mixing it up with the chocolate till it was one big mess. That wasn't like her. She liked to eat the topping first, from the bottom up. What was she doing mixing it all up till it didn't look fit to eat?

"I'm not hungry," she said and got up from the table.

"Theresa, wait." I paid the bill and caught up with her as she breezed out the door. "What's the matter?" I asked. "You act like this is my fault."

She walked fast. "Course it ain't your fault," she said. "I gotta get home."

"What you mean, you gotta get home? We just got here."

We fought all the way back. I seen her to the door, said good night, and didn't get no kiss or nothing. That was that.

At church the next morning, I waited for her like usual by the front door, but she came in already hooked arm-in-arm with none other than Johnny G, my youngest pupil. Don't know what made him such a good catch. Wondered if he found out yet how old she was and if she knew how young he was.

That evening at supper, Johnny G didn't meet my eye or say nothing. Everybody else chattered away like it didn't make no difference that Theresa had gone from one of us to the next. He and I never did talk about it. What was the point? Happened all the time. Hell, hadn't I done that with Carlin and the rest? And wouldn't I do it again?

They put the school in an old storefront near the church. Children went in the daytime, adults at night. Without my job as teacher, I had no way to pay for living at the men's club. Plus, there wasn't nothing special 'bout me no more. I wasn't no dandy, wasn't no ladies' man.

"You don't have to go, Jeb," Pastor Amos said. "Stay and tutor if you like."

"Nah, that's all right," I said. "I gotta find me a paying job. Thanks anyway."

I didn't want to see Theresa and Johnny G together, so I quit going to church too. That whole life was over for me.

I was out on the street.

CHAPTER 18

1866

SHANTYTOWN

I thought life was only about getting through it.
—J. Johnson

I was tired, pure and simple—tired of moving, tired of trying, tired of working so hard. And for what?

The day I left the men's home, I walked down the street past the ice cream parlor, the park, and everything that had been home. The farther I went into the city, the more rundown it got. I came to an area near the tracks filled with tents and shacks full of brothers and sisters, like where I grew up.

The difference was like day and night, though. These people lived by the fire real primitive-like. None had a steady job. Trains passed all the time, bringing new brothers and sisters, while others crawled onto the slow-moving freight cars and left. The noise of the locomotives helped cover the sounds of crying and fighting here, but nothing could cover up the stink. We burned anything we could to keep warm, even things not meant to burn. And our sanitation system? The river nearby.

Sickness and stench were something you got hardened to after a while. You just didn't feel the sickness or smell the stink, and you stopped hearing the noise.

That wasn't true of the cold, though. I never knew cold like we had my first winter there—cold so bad it hurt. I'd been in Cleveland one winter already in the church house, and we didn't hardly go out when it was bad. Here, we lived outside. There were only a few ways to keep warm—by the fire if you were lucky, by a woman if you were luckier, and by whiskey if you could afford it.

I survived by doing plant work, and not the kind you grow in the ground. Before dawn, we'd crowd the fences at factories, trying to look our best, which wasn't saying much. In the dark, they—mostly foremen—came to the fence to hire workers.

One day, we were all lined up against the fence single file, so they could see each of us. But as the foremen came close to one spot, everybody on the ends of the line crowded towards the middle. These foremen looked right past those pushed up against the fence to the taller, bigger men behind.

"I'll take you and you and you," the big guy with a pencil stuck behind his ear said.

"And I'll take you four right here, and you three over there," said the other.

The rest of us dragged ourselves back to our screaming women and quieting booze.

Maybe it was my spectacles or the intelligent look I tried to keep in my eye, but I got picked a lot at first. The pay was all right cause we did tough work nobody else wanted to do. Happy to get paid at the end of a long day, I took mine right to the grocery before it closed, coming home with a ham for everybody and special treats in my pockets for me and my lady of the day—or night, I should say.

After a while, I thought about the sit-yation. My dream was for us Negroes to pull together and serve our own, but here I was, depending on the white man once again—something I told myself I'd never do. Feeling low, I hit the bottle pretty hard that night.

"You think too much," said Taylor at the fire. "Just be glad to get work."

"There has to be another way," I said, looking around. "Even here."

"Hey," said Charlie from across the fire, "we do the best we can. So do you."

I felt a nudge, and two arms stretched over my shoulders from behind and slid down my chest as Rosie, my lady, came up and leaned down, bringing her cheek close to mine. "Don't you think it's time for bed, sugar?"

She was hard to resist, but I pulled away. I needed to figure this out.

"Dawn comes early for working men," she said.

"I'll get there."

Miffed, she turned and disappeared back to her shanty.

Taylor waved his bottle at her. "Better get it while the getting's good."

Not up to loving, I stayed and drank, but felt even lower when I finally hauled myself back to her place and found the door locked. I looked up at the night sky. Failure set in.

Charlie, on his way to his place, stopped to do his business. Leaning left, his stream hit her shanty. "Guess you're outta luck," he laughed. He pulled hisself together and staggered away. "Come on," he said waving me into his place.

I didn't make it to work call the following morning or the next. Instead, I slept in, ate, and stayed at the fire into the night with others who didn't work, trying to figure it out between swigs of suds. I thought about schooling some of them here, but looking around, I decided they were so far from learning, it would never happen. Cleaning up, I quit drinking and showed up at a few offices to make my skills known.

At one place, I presented myself at the front desk, standing tall, hat in hand.

The lady looked up. "May I help you?"

I'd worked real hard on what to say and how to say it. "I'd like to offer my services," I said. "I can read, write, and figure real good. Was a teacher up at the church."

"Is that right? Well I'm sorry, we've got plenty of that kind of help."

I looked around the office at the other workers—men with green shades over their eyes. Women worked there too, but no one of color. Why humiliate myself trying at more places? They were all the same.

Good thing the brothers shared, even if they hardly had nothing. Some brewed pretty good hooch and made their living selling it to the brothers. Others would fade into the night and slink back before dawn, their pockets full. These didn't share, though. Instead, the next day, they'd be at the pawnshop, getting what they could or walking up and down the business district selling watches and baubles hung on the insides of their coats.

Surprising how many people bought stolen goods. It didn't faze them, though they had to know. The deal was too good to be lawful, which made the buyers thieves too, since they kept the takers in business.

At first, the only theft I was guilty of was stealing women. They'd give me that look when they'd be with their man at the fire, and I'd return it—you know the look I'm talking about—and sure enough, soon I'd be in someone else's bed. She might switch to me as her man for a while, maybe not. Usually a fight was involved.

There came a time when I did find a woman of my own, though—Miss Lucy, a servant maid from Chattanooga. Met her at the fire my first spring in Shantytown. Pretty? Nah, but good—oh my, yes sirree Bob. Miss Lucy had other admirers and one morning after going out for work call, I came back to find one of them in my place in her shanty. Had it out with both of them, then dumped her after I whupped him. People underrate a person with a disability. I got the best of him cause of it.

After Miss Lucy came Miss Millie and after her a string of ladies to keep my mind off of what I was doing. Or wasn't doing. We was always fighting and bickering and laughing and having us a time.

One winter, it was so cold, and me and my woman—Jemma now—had nothing to eat, nothing but rags to wear, nothing to keep us warm but each other. Weak from no food, she got a hacking cough. I knew I had to do something or we were both gonna freeze to death. Folks died from the cold every winter. I didn't want us to be next.

Now, I swore I'd never steal after what happened in that
farmhouse years before. But we were a long way from there,
and I plum forgot what it was like to be so hungry. Keeping my
morals straight just didn't seem to count when death stared us
in the face.

It began with little jaunts, keeping watch while others did
the dirty work. Then one time I got me a chance to grab a
bauble or two. We weren't in nobody's home, just somebody's
shop. In fact, we stole from one pawnshop and sold it to
another. Piece of cake. Sometimes some got caught, but I
didn't.

One time though, Evil Jimmy and I were out on a lark,
catching ourselves a few things at a jewelry store. An alarm
went off, but we got out with full sacks over our backs before
anyone got there. We scurried down an alley before we stopped
and dropped our bags. Bent over, our hands on our knees, we
caught our breath.

"Whew!" he said.

I waited till I caught mine and answered, "That was close."

"Let's see what we got."

We loosened the drawstrings and emptied our potato sacks.

"Now our pockets," he said.

We emptied them. My pile was bigger than his.

"We even-steven on this, right?" he said, eyeing my stuff.

"Yeah," I said, looking over the loot. "We sure got a lot."

"Looks like you got more than me," he said.

"Sure does." I thought how all these baubles would trans-
late into groceries and medicine. "We done real good."

He reached for a large woman's brooch from my pile.
"Think I'll have me that doodad right there to even it up."

I needed every bit to get me and Jemma out of our mess
back at camp. Grabbing his wrist, I said, "We even-steven going
in and coming out, but what we get is our own. You said it
yourself, 'finders-keepers.'"

He pulled away. "No, man. You got that wrong."

"You said we each grab what looks good to us."

"That don't mean it's yours to keep."

I stood. "Sure as hell does."

He was up too and grabbed me by the collar. "We's even-steven, fifty-fifty."

I chopped at him with my arm. Going down hard, he hit his head on a cement step and lay still. A dark red pool started to spread on the ground below his head.

I looked around and didn't see nobody. Stuffing our booty into my bag, I ran for it. Returning to camp, I skulked to our lean-to and crawled in next to Jemma, my bag at my back.

We hadn't told nobody about our plans to go out that evening. That had been part of the deal. When they found Evil Jimmy missing, nobody would know he had been with me.

I pawned it all the next day. The police came asking questions, but nobody knew nothing.

From then on, I did my looting alone. Never drove no automobile or had a good job. All of us in Shantytown lived by making the best of what we had and stealing what we didn't. We took what we needed and were good at it. Cops came along every night and rightfully so, cause the skullduggery was fierce in them parts. The women were never safe—we either fought each other over them or fought the women over other men.

It was hell.

I never did marry. Jemma bore me three children, but I couldn't stand having them nearby and was no good to them. Bossed them around and made them cry cause I felt so bad myself. Hit them, in fact. I was bad, real bad.

One night, winters later, I sat by the fire warming my fingers when I felt a sharp object in the middle of my back. Somebody leaned up against me from behind. A deep voice vibrated into my soul.

"Don't say nothing," he said. "Get up real slow."

Nobody took notice as I rose and followed him, another brother following me. Knew who it was by his walk. Been keeping my eye out for him. In a way, I knew this was coming.

He took me over by the tracks, then turned on me. His blade flashed in the starlight. The other brother faded back to the fire.

"We gonna settle this once and for all," he said, crouching down, his blade weaving S patterns in front of him. "Just the two of us."

We circled each other, both down low now. I tried to get lower so I could get my knife out of my boot.

"I seen you take everybody's woman some time or another." A quick move forward with a sideways slash.

I sucked in my gut. He missed by inches.

"Knew you'd be after mine, sooner or later."

He lunged forward and got me across the rib cage.

My arm held the wound as we danced a circle.

"Been waiting for the moment, and it done come."

He lunged and thrust.

My reactions slower cause of my wound and the booze, his blade slid clear into my chest. I felt a searing pain and went down, my arms wrapped round myself.

He stood over me. "Never trusted you," he said and kicked me in the side. "You don't deserve to live." He came straight down and stabbed me in the throat, then left me by the tracks to die.

I looked up at the stars and wondered why I hadn't noticed more how pretty they were, now that I wouldn't see them no more.

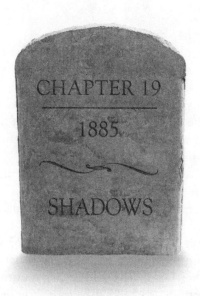

CHAPTER 19

1885

SHADOWS

It will come. Just don't think you know how it's gonna happen.
—J. Johnson

Remembering all this didn't solve nothing. Here I was now, back with the same old problem. Except for Old Horace and Jessie, I had no one to talk to and felt more like an outcast than ever.

I didn't really know how bad off I was till I got up from my tree stump and walked over to little Jessie, who stood like always in the field.

"Jessie."

She was all into her head and was gone—really gone.

"Jessie, talk to me."

Her eyes focused on me and widened.

"Jessie, what's wrong?"

She tried to speak.

I went to take her by the shoulders. She woke all the way and jumped back.

"Jessie, it's me—Jeb."

She held out her hands to stop me.

"I ain't gonna hurt you, honey. I just wanna know . . ."

"Stay away!" she screamed, fear in her eyes. She knew it was me. I could tell.

"Jessie, honey," I said soft-like, so she wouldn't be afraid. "It's me, Jeb. The one you came to see the first night I died."

Fists to her mouth, she held herself real tight.

"Jessie, don't be a-scared of me."

"I can't talk to you any more," she breathed.

"What? Who told you that?"

"You're different. You're a dark one. You make me feel different inside, and I can't talk to you."

"Oh hell, you gonna give me that guff too? I'm just me—Jeb. We had some good talks, you and me. What changed?"

She shook her head, fists still at her mouth. "You've got trouble all around you so bad I can see it. You're dangerous."

I stepped forward and she screamed.

Pans and tin plates clattered as everyone by the fire jumped between us.

Dolores stood in front of me. "Stay aWAY from her, hear?"

"You're no good!" said Shamus.

Winston picked Jessie up and held her. "There, there," he murmured.

She wrapped her arms tight around his neck and looked to her mama's home as they walked back to the fire.

"Best advice is just stay away from him," he told her. "He bother you again, just . . ." His voice faded.

I backed to the edge of the forest and sat down. I really was all alone.

Or not.

Hearing movement behind me, I was up and over to them before they were even out of the woods.

The big white fella spoke first. "Well, look who's here."

"You ready to join up?" asked the big dark woman I couldn't hardly see.

I looked over at the group by the fire. "None of them will talk to me, except old Horace," I said.

"And he ain't gonna be around much longer, anyway," said the blonde boy.

The dark lady jabbed him. "Hush up, Amos."

He scowled.

"What do you mean?" I asked.

She sighed, cocked her head, then looked at the big white man. "He ain't ready."

He nodded. "Right again, Jelilah. Let's go."

I jumped in front. "Tell me why you won't stay and talk to me."

"You're not ready to join us, so we're moving on," said Jelilah, linking her arm through the big white guy's. "C'mon, Harold."

They led a parade of maybe seven or ten—several more than the other night—and passed me by.

"All right," I said, grabbing my hat, "I'm a-coming."

Soon as I joined up, we moved on, gliding above the road. No walking or running or skipping or hopping. No more limping around for this old ghost. We glided, oh yes indeedy, we glided.

Ghosts—that's what we were, of course—came and went with this group. Shadows were marked by a cloud of misery so dense you could see it. When you're alive, you hide it. The minute you die, it's there for all to see.

I went with the Shadows cause nobody else cared. At least *they* came around to be with me. They were like me, only they knew more about all this. It wasn't a hard decision to make.

I let them take the reins. What did I know? Everybody said I had to learn the ropes.

Some things hit me wrong right off, though, but I didn't say nothing. That's usually a mistake.

"So where we going?" I asked Amos.

"To find the next one," he whispered, looking ahead.

"The next one what?"

The whole group stopped. Weird. I didn't even think about stopping, and we all just stopped at once.

Jelilah turned around and pointed at me. "You," she said. The group split wide apart to let her through. She jabbed at me, and I backed up. "You're lucky we came back."

Amos stepped in front of me. "Jelilah, don't."

She whacked him a good one. "Shut up!" she said and turned back to me. "NEVER say nothing when we's hunting, hear?"

I nodded and we were off again, Jelilah in front, the kid bringing up the rear. We glided along faster than I could move by myself, whooshing over hill and dale in the dark of the night.

Coming to a little town, we slowed to take a look. Jelilah spotted something to the left. We shifted that way and came to a halt in front of a cigar store where some poor fellow, dark as could be, sat on a bench by a door, staring at nothing.

He noticed us and sat up. "You can see me?"

"Anybody else around here we'd be looking at?" asked Jelilah.

He pulled his hat off his head and held it to his chest with both hands. "No, ma'am."

"You done sitting here like this?" she asked.

"What are you saying?"

"Want to join up with us?"

He looked at the rest of us, then back at her. "Where are you going?"

"That don't matter. We're going. You coming?" She started off and we moved with her.

"Wait!" he cried.

We halted, he caught up, and away we went. As we slid out of town, I looked over at Homer, who stared ahead, glassy-eyed.

After a minute, he looked back at me. "He's a new one."

"You mean he just died?"

"Uh-huh."

Nobody worried about where we were headed. Jelilah took care of steering us. We were just along for the ride.

A group mindset is scary. You agree on small things first, then on big things. Pretty soon, you don't have your own way about you no more. Shadows were even more like that. With Shadows, if one of us went off the deep end, we all did.

"Homer, how long you been doing this?"

He gazed at me. "How long?" He looked ahead again, the thought working at him. "How does anyone know how long you do anything any more?"

"Shut up!" Jelilah yelled.

We were on a mission to get the next soul that might not even know he was a Shadow yet. Jelilah could sniff them out like a dog. We'd slow down, look around, and sure enough, there'd be a Shadow so dark you could hardly see inside it, and I ain't talking skin color. I'm talking about a shadow that don't show on the ground. A shadow no light can take away. A shadow that hangs on you like a dark cloud.

Shadows weren't so hard to be around though. Jelilah had a good side. But hell, when you think on it, even murderers got a good side. That don't make them good. Some of the others, like Homer, hardly ever talked. Fact was, hardly any of us talked.

We ran that night without finding another soul. By dawn, we were tuckered and slowed to a stop in a forest. Everybody got off, kind of like getting off a wagon. The others all found places to rest till it was just the new man and me standing there. I was tired before we'd even begun. Now I couldn't hardly move. We looked at each other, then parted and found ourselves a space to rest.

When I awoke, the sun had already set. Everyone stood and stretched.

In a moment, we were off again. Staying to the back of the pack, I followed, watching everybody else.

We hadn't been out long before Jelilah held up her hand. We stopped, got off, split up for some reason, and scrambled for cover.

"Y'all get back out here. NOW!" she yelled.

In an instant we were beside her.

"Sissies!" she laughed. "Just cause somebody's coming, y'all run and hide. Hmph!"

In a heartbeat—a saying ghosts don't take lightly—another band of Shadows moved by so fast, we nearly didn't see them till they slowed and circled back, then stopped in front of Jelilah. Must have been at least fifty of them.

A huge man stepped forward. "Well."

"Well, hell," said Jelilah.

"This is our place."

Jelilah looked around. "Ain't no sign saying so."

Suddenly, they were all around us.

"You're in the wrong place, lady."

Jelilah laughed. "Story of my life!" She stopped laughing. "But not now. Nobody tells me, or mine,"—she looked at us— "where we can or can't be."

His group moved in tighter. "No?"

"No!" But we hightailed it and didn't stop for a long time, moving so fast, everything went by in a blur. Don't know how, but we stayed together real tight.

When we did stop, we fell out of the group and groped around for places to lie down. That was it for the night.

I never got to ask nobody nothing. Every time I woke up, we all woke and got going. With no time for talk, I could only watch and figure things for myself.

I saw that Jelilah didn't like ghosts that weren't Shadows. We called them "white" ghosts or "Clearies." Clearies didn't like Shadows either. Being near us made them real tired and achy, same as the Living.

One night, we found a white ghost sitting by hisself gazing at nothing, like when you watch your life go by. Jelilah sat down and put her arm across his shoulder real nice-like.

"Hi," she said, mussing his hair.

He came out of it real slow. When he turned and saw who was being so friendly, his eyes just about bulged out of their sockets. We had to wait quite a while for Jelilah to get over that laughing spell.

Going out made us real tired, and ghosts are tired to begin with. By then I knew that the more Shadows we had, the more energy we had. But on this night, we ended up back where we started with nobody new to show for it.

"Homer," I said, as I lay down on a bunch of dead leaves.

He looked over from his resting spot.

"How long you been with this bunch?" I'd asked him before, but he never would answer.

"Long enough," he said.

What's he mean? I wondered.

"Means I been with this group long enough to know that we don't talk to each other."

I looked at him funny.

He smiled. "We hear thoughts real good. You'll get so you do too."

"Homer!" Jelilah yelled. "Get over here."

He whisked to her side.

"What you doing, talking like that?" she asked.

"Like what?"

"You know we don't do that round here."

Homer shrugged.

Jelilah, angry, disappeared.

What's this all about? I wondered.

She was back and in my face. "WHAT? What?" she asked. "You hang round us long enough you'll know what's what. And what's what is we don't listen to each other's thoughts, that's what. Hear?"

I nodded.

Later, young Amos explained. "Once you get so you hear everybody's thoughts, you have to pretend you don't hear some things, that's all."

"But I *don't* hear them," I said. And I didn't—then.

One night not long after, I sat alongside Ben, a new one we'd picked up a few nights before.

I ain't so sure 'bout this, I heard him say.

"Me neither," I answered.

He looked at me.

"Jeb!"

You didn't dawdle when Jelilah called. I slid over to her. "Yes?"

I could hardly see her eyes as they narrowed in the moonlight. "What you think you're doing?"

"Nothing," I said. "Just having a little chat with Ben over there."

"You think so, huh?"

I nodded.

"Well, that AIN'T what's happening," she said. "You're answering his thoughts, that's what you're doing. Didn't I tell you never to do that?"

I didn't get it.

I know this boy ain't stupid, I heard her say to herself.

"I *ain't* stupid," I said. "And I ain't no 'boy.'"

That did it. She tore round the place like a whirlwind, busting down tree limbs big as your thigh, then turned to the whole group, who were on their feet now, ready to move if they had to.

"Ain't nobody reading *nobody's* thoughts!" she said. "Everybody understand?"

"Oh yes, ma'am," I heard.

"Sure," said another.

"No mind-reading," said somebody else.

Did I read someone's mind?

"Course you did. You answered him back when he didn't say nothing to you at all," Jelilah said. She'd just done what she didn't want us to do, but I kept my mouth shut and my mind still and there weren't no problems after that.

I knew why Jelilah didn't want us reading minds, though. She wanted to think nobody could hear hers, cause when it got right down to it, Jelilah was stupid.

Think we'll go that way, she thought one night when we got to a junction.

I checked to see if anybody else heard what I had. Every face was blank. I looked down the road to the right, then to the left. We could go over hill and dale if we wanted to, but it was easier if we went down roads already cleared. Besides, we wanted to stay low, where Shadows might be hiding out.

She looked to the right. *We'll go that way,* she thought. Then she looked to the left. *Or maybe that way.*

The woman didn't know what she was doing. I didn't think this in words, just ideas, cause I didn't want her to hear my thoughts.

She led by pure power. Sheer will controlled our puny little minds so none of us had to think for ourselves. I wondered if that ever happened anytime in my life. Gave a person something to think on—if you had a mind to, that is.

Once I seen she really wasn't all that smart, I was more on the alert. You never knew. Another group of Shadows with a nastier leader might be around the next corner.

I learned to tune out just about everything I didn't want to hear. Otherwise, the noise was too much. Listening is not done with the ear anyway. It's done on the inside.

I learned one thing for sure in all this. When you're living, your thoughts are not just your own, especially thoughts that come out of the blue like birds flying around, landing on different trees. They sing their song, then move on. That's what thoughts are like. Now, that tree can dwell on that song or let it pass by. People are like that. You can just let it pass through and it's just meaningless jibber-jabber. But take a thought and make it into something, then you're a Creator, making something out of nothing.

Me? I had just rolled through life, just like I rolled along with this Jelilah group now.

One time she decided we were going out in the daytime. Daylight hurt and we usually stayed out of it. But this being a cloudy day, she thought we might stir up some trouble. So we cruised into town and set around an old dry goods store, watching people go in and out. We played tricks on the Living just cause we could. Y'all don't realize how all your thoughts are out there for everyone to hear. I didn't know it when I was alive either, but I sure learned about it after I died. Yes, I did.

An old lady that couldn't hardly walk caught Jelilah's attention as she tried to step up on the boardwalk in front of a store. Jelilah went over and blocked the lady's step with her foot. Every time that woman tried to step up, Jelilah stuck out her leg so she couldn't.

Why, I can't even get up onto the boardwalk any more, thought the lady. She looked up and down the street. Nobody seen her trouble. Her shoulders slumped. *Guess I need a cane after all.* She looked so sad. With all the people passing by you'd think somebody would have helped that old woman. But they didn't. Nobody helped.

"Yeah, lady," said Jelilah. "You're going downhill."

I'm going downhill, the old lady thought. *Just too old to get out anymore.* She turned and hobbled away.

Jelilah laughed. So did everybody else.

Not me. This was downright mean. In fact, most everything we did was mean. We were nothing but a bunch of mean
old bullies.

Finally, one day as the group got ready to go, I decided to
take a break.

"Jeb," said Jelilah, "time to go."

"I ain't going," says I.

No discussion, no argument, nothing from them.

Off they went. But don't you know they came around
again to see me sitting right where they left me.

"You coming?" said Jelilah. She waited a minute, then
cocked her head. "You know, Jeb, if you ain't with us, you're
against us."

"I ain't against you," I said. "I just don't want to do it no
more."

They waited.

"Just leave me here," says I. "I'm tired."

They left.

After going inside myself for a long, long time, I surfaced
and looked around. Where was I, anyway? I remembered seeing a sign as we roamed around a few nights before I dropped
out of the group. "North Carolina," it said. We never paid
attention to boundaries and state lines. Didn't matter which
state we were in anymore. There was no government on this
side, except for the government of your own Interior.

I decided to go into the nearest town where a few others
like me leaned against storefronts or stretched out on benches.
It wasn't a "good" part of town, and everybody just rolled
around inside their heads all day long.

Now let me tell you, if you mull things over and over like
we did, you never get nowhere. You just see it all the same again
and again. Sure, you might figure some things out by yourself,
but there are ideas just a-waiting to come to you if you give
them a little space inside your head.

For entertainment, I watched the Living. I'd see happy people and feel sorry for them cause of the pain that was bound to
happen to them. *Everybody gets sick and dies,* I thought. I didn't
know about the kind of happiness that lasts; I didn't understand health as a never-ending way of being. Didn't know you

could do that. It comes from your insides, and you can hold
onto it no matter what, cause you're true to the very core of
your being. It's the bad that's temporary, but I didn't know that
either.

Watching people get tossed around by life made me sadder
than I already was, so I went deeper inside. But I didn't like
what was there either, so I found a place halfway in between.
Once in a while I came out for a breather, but it was so dark
around me all the time. I did see something, though. . . .

This one little girl. A man walked behind her a ways, like he
was stalking her. I just knew what was gonna happen, and it
wouldn't be good. Remembering how the Jelilah group yelled
into people's minds, I thought, *Maybe I can change this sit-
yation.*

Now how you gonna do that? I asked myself.

I'm gonna tell the man not to do it.

Oh you are, huh? I answered. *He's gonna do what he's gonna
do.*

I can tell her to watch out for that man.

What's she gonna do? I argued. *She's all by herself walking
home from school.*

An old woman tended her garbage down the street. Maybe
she could help.

No, I thought as I watched her mutter to herself. *She's all
closed up in her own thinking. I'll never get through.*

A man passing by looked to be a good sort. I sidled up and
yelled in his ear, "That little girl over there shouldn't be walking all by herself. Could be dangerous."

The man looked out the corner of his eye and seen the little girl. I heard him think, *Hmm. Dangerous for that little girl all
by herself.*

Singing a little song, she strolled along unmindful of everyone and everything.

That's dangerous, he thought.

I yelled in his ear, "Someone could come along and hurt
her."

Someone could come and hurt her, he thought, then looked
around and spied the other man watching her so close he didn't
see this man spying him from the other side of the street. The

good man seen this, and you know what he did? He walked right across that street and put hisself between the girl and the stalker.

The little girl seen this new man getting close. She walked faster, and he kept right up.

The old man farther back thought, *How can I get around this guy?*

Everybody walked faster, the new man staying between the others.

Two boys playing on the sidewalk noticed her coming up the street. "Hey, Sherilee!"

"Hey, Derek two-face!" she answered.

Laughing, they joined her and kept going on down the street.

The new man didn't let up. It bothered him still—and it bothered me. I seen this kind of thing happen every day around here. Nothing good ever came of it. He turned around and seen the other guy still stalking the little one. Stopping in his tracks, he turned and faced the stalker.

"Get outta here!" he said.

The other man slowed.

"Keep your hands off her, you slimy sonofabitch," said my friend. "Anything ever happens to her, I'll know who did it."

The other man stopped. "You don't know me."

"You keep your hands off her," said the good man. Then he turned around and followed the children. The other man went away.

I caught up to the good man and yelled, "Tell her to take another way home!"

Sherilee turned up the walk to what must have been her house and went inside. He followed right up to the door and knocked.

Her mama came to the door, her hands on her hips. "Well?" she asked.

"I seen your girl walk home today," he said. "A man followed her, and I got between them to make sure nothing happened."

The woman's hand moved to her heart.

"Tell her she better not walk alone or take that way home no more," he said. "Bad man there." He shook his head. "*Bad man.*"

The mama called, "Sherilee!"

Sherilee came to the door, looked up to her mama and said, "That's the man that followed me home. He scared me."

He said, "Little girl, ain't me that should be scaring you. Another man followed you too. I got between you both, but you only seen me and walked faster. Good thing, cause you shouldn't trust no one you don't know. I went faster too, because he kept up behind me." He bent to look in her face. "Little girl, I just want you to know, that man wasn't up to no good."

She hid in her mother's dress, her finger in her mouth.

"Take another way home from now on. Don't go that way no more. And don't walk alone. You didn't see him, but I did."

He tipped his hat and left. They watched him walk down the street. Then Sherilee looked up at her mama who shook her head at little Sherilee, picked her up, and held her tight.

As the man walked away, I went up and said, "You did a good thing today. Yes, sir. You maybe saved a little girl's life."

He looked up at how sunny the day was, breathed in the air, smiled, and walked on. I looked back at the little girl's house and then up at the sky too, and noticed that it seemed a mite bluer. Yes, it did.

Just a mite bluer.

CHAPTER 20

1935

HELPING

He's there, a-sittin' and a-waitin' for the moment when you finally see that yes, this is His world, His game.
—J. Johnson

If I could get through to people like that, maybe I could help and mean something in this world after all.

I couldn't undo the bad I already done from hanging around bad people. That was what I done wrong in life, more than anything else—staying around bad people without trying to change things. I let them get away with murder, to tell you the truth. Hanging with them made them stronger too. It's true what they say about strength in numbers. That's how Jelilah got her power. Fed off us like a parasite. If the rest of us had thought for ourselves, she would have been nothing.

I started to think on all I done and should have done, and it made me sick. But I wasn't that way no more. No sir. I could do things. I could change things and make a difference. So every once in a while I'd come out of hibernation and watch the goings-on amongst the Living.

One day, I seen a man picking pockets and said to myself, *Mm, mm, mmm! Now, how I gonna stop that?*

A cop nearby swung a billy club back and forth, not seeing nothing. I went over and said in his ear, "Looky that guy over there. Don't he look shifty?"

The cop seen the man and thought, *This guy looks mighty suspicious.*

"Better keep an eye on him," I said.

I better keep an eye on him, he thought.

Quick as a wink, that pickpocket got somebody's wallet and ran off to see what was in it.

Get him! I yelled.

"Stop! Police!" he called, but the pickpocket disappeared. The cop started after him, but stopped. He had to stay on his beat.

For me though, it was a beginning. I'd see pickpockets and race to get to their next victim before they did.

"Better put your wallet in a safer place," I said to one.

Looking around, he pulled his wallet from his back pocket and stuffed it into the inner breast pocket of his coat.

"*There's* one ready to give somebody the slip," I said another day to a policeman.

The cop looked and sure enough, it happened.

Playing cops and robbers, I realized I could be around other ghosts and people too, and nobody got sick no more. Now why was that? I heard everything real clear now too.

I seen the same pickpockets all the time in places like the stadium at a big college in North Carolina. They had games almost every week, and when the crowds were real tight, I'd float above and watch these guys. It's hard to see, but if you've got an eagle eye, you won't miss it. I'd spot one, tell the cops, and watch them catch him.

After a while, though, it began to feel like a lost cause. Times were changing. There were more people and more automobiles, aeroplanes, and diesel trains to move them faster. More stations full of people and the pickpockets that went with these places. Big crowded stores made for robbers. There would always be pickpockets and robbers.

There's got to be more I can do than this.

CHAPTER 21

1995

CONNECTIONS

Ask for help. Then let it come to you.
—J. Johnson

After a while, I came up with an answer.

Hospitals! One was close by. I flew over and walked through its doors.

What a shock! Spirits all over the place! And none of them looked like they knew if they were coming or going.

I hung around a while—might have been weeks, I don't know. This place got me real tired, and I had to take me lots of rests. Sometimes it got real quiet, then all of a sudden, everybody would be running back and forth. Then it quieted again.

It was interesting, I'll say that. I learned a lot too. All these patients hooked up to wires and newfangled gadgets to keep them alive. Their bodies were there for the living to see, but their spirits roamed the hallways, bumping into each other and streaming through everyone else.

Friends and family from the Other Side stood round their beds, a-waiting for the Grand Come-over. But no, some operation or machine or "procedure" came along to make patients fit enough to be kept half alive for who-knows-why. They were miserable, and so were the folks hanging around waiting on both sides.

So why are they all hooked up? I wanted to know. *Why don't they just let them go, for God's sake?* By then, I seen enough folks die and zoom right to the Light to know that's the place to be. Nobody else could go into their Light. Some tried, but it was just for the one.

I got into a few discussions with folks from the Other Side—I call it the "O.S." You might call it "Heaven." And yes, they come back and forth all the time a-helping and comforting the Living. Biggest time to see them was when somebody was getting ready to die.

Pretty interesting here at the hospital—the ones from the O.S. seeing me and me seeing them, like it was no big deal. Happened all the time. Something you got used to after a while. Strange, ain't it? I got used to seeing them come and go like it was normal.

In some ways, I guess it was.

And then there were them that died but didn't cross over— the Shadows like me, and the Clearies. I learned that most of the clear ones could go but didn't know it.

I began asking them Clearies, "What you wanna do? You wanna go or you wanna stay?" They looked at me like I was the fool. Maybe so.

Let me say here, a lot of time must have passed since I died, cause things were real modern now—gadgets and ways of living I didn't understand at first. I learned fast though. When they said "Code Blue!" I knew it wasn't good—from their standpoint—somebody was going or was already gone. So every once in a while, when I heard the beepers go off, I drifted in to see what was really going on.

First time, everyone was frantically working on a body while the poor guy floated overhead. Nobody even saw the glow in the corner, so I yelled, "Go to the Light! Go to the Light!"

Nurses, doctors, and aides scrambled around. Meanwhile, there he was, peaceful as could be, watching the crowd fuss over his body.

When somebody new from the O.S. floated in next to him, the fella looked and his face lit up like sunshine. The new guy took him by the hand, led him into the Light and that was that.

Never knew if he heard me yelling about going to the Light or not. *Some don't need no help,* I thought. *No sirree Bob.*

Weighing everything I just seen, a thought came from out of the blue as they covered the body and wheeled it out.

I gots my own Light, I told myself, *I just have to find it.*

Or maybe it would find me.

I had the best chance of helping the dazed and confused ones whose bodies were dead but the machines held them here. They weren't really ghosts—their spirits stood by their beds or watched others hooked up to machines, just like them. They even walked around in pairs, sharing the same problem.

What problem? Well, tarnation! They weren't here, and they sure as hell weren't there.

"You see the Light?" I asked an old man wandering the halls one night. Must have been about eighty—old enough to have finished what he came to do. Time to go. "You don't want to hang around here no more," I told him. "Go to the Light."

Dreamy-eyed, he turned to me, then started to talk. "I don't know. My family's here, and I want to see what they do with my body. . . ."

"They gonna throw your body in the ground one way or another is what they're gonna do," I told him. "You don't want to see it get burned up."

"They won't do that. I didn't want cremation."

"You don't know what they gonna do. Some living folk think that what happens after you die is their business, not yours. They gonna do it their way, since you dead and gone."

He looked at me. "But I'm . . ."

"At least they think you gone."

He looked less dreamy, more worried.

"Don't matter what they do with that rotten old body," I said.

That got him mad.

"Look," I said, "you don't need it no more. You got a right good body now—way better than the one in that-there bed."

A long loud beep came from his room and we rushed in. Everybody ran helter-skelter. Finally, though, they covered him up and took him away. The poor guy followed his dead old body down to the guts of the building, and I went along. Might as well keep him company. We waited beside his corpse all night. Next day, they took it to another place and dumped it in a box. They shoved it right into that big old furnace and it turned to flames as they slid the door closed.

"They promised!" he cried, jumping all about. "They promised me they wouldn't." He got real angry—feelings he never would have had to feel if he had gone to the Light in the first place.

It still waited. I couldn't see it, but he could.

Folks get all riled up when they stay around too long watching what happens with their bodies or belongings or their children or houses and property. They hang around just like I did, just like this one here did, and get hooked—always wanting to know what's gonna happen next. Then they get to be ghosts. That's how it happens for some.

I don't know if I had a Light to go to at first. Too busy watching the goings-on around me and feeling melancholy, I never seen it if it was there. And now this man hung around here when he could have been long gone.

Wore ... me ... out.

Something about this one nurse at the hospital—she went about her business not saying much, but you could tell that, deep down inside, she had a thought or two of her own. She wasn't persnickety like some, but she knew what was going on.

She had a problem with people dying and not being able to do nothing about it. She couldn't see that dying was just part of living. Plus, life got her down in the dumps, and she couldn't see that maybe it was better that everybody dies anyway.

One day, I slid over to her. "Lady," I said, "you ain't got it so bad."

Sitting at a table in their little "commissary," she looked out the window and drank a soda.

"Compared to some, your problems ain't nothing. For one thing, you're white. That's a start, cause you got it easier than some."

She sighed.

I got up and walked round front of her. "Lady, you alive. Look what you can do, girl. You talk to patients and they hear you. You listen to their problems and comfort them."

She picked up her things with another sigh. I followed her back to her floor. She got to that station where nurses work.

Another nurse looked up as she walked in and said, "Have a good time?"

"What?" she said. "On my break?"

The woman smiled.

"Oh, yeah." She rolled her eyes. "Sure. A real party."

I followed her down the hall. "Miss," I said, "we can have a real good time, you and me, if you just listen."

Shooing me away like a thought she didn't want to hear, she walked into a room. The patient—a big woman 'bout the nurse's age—lay on her side, bawling without a sound. A girl in the other bed lay fast asleep. Wrapped up in her own troubles, my nursie checked the lady's machine, her bag under the bed, and looked at the tubes.

"Now, lady," I said. "Ain't you gonna say nothing to cheer her up?"

She made a few notes on a clipboard hanging off the end of the bed.

"Look at her," says I.

Finally, she did.

"Bawling like she ain't got nothing left to live for."

She put her hand on the blanket over the woman's foot. "You okay, hon?"

"That's the way." I'd been watching this-here nurse. Usually, she was good with patients—keeping them happy with her cheery, understanding ways. Don't know what got into her on this night, but she was coming out of it now. Yes, she was.

I helped her do it too. Sure as anything, I did.

The woman blew her nose on a tissue my little (she wasn't that little, really) nurse handed her. "Oh," she said between sniffs, "I just got the news."

"It's a tough one, isn't it?" said Nursie.

"I had no idea," said the lady. "Came on so fast." Her eyes teared up. "Caught me by surprise. I just didn't know. . . ." And with that, she was bawling all over again.

Nursie sat down, put her arm around the woman's shoulders, and danged if that lady didn't come into my nursie's arms and cry and cry.

There's some things you can't change. But you can make them a little better just by being there when it happens. Yes, you can.

I walked out of that room a happier man.

Another time, she was leaving the hospital for the day—night, actually. She worked the night shift. By the time she was going home, the rest of the world was coming to work.

Anyhow, she was leaving, and I was alongside. "You gonna have a great day today, Miss."

She laughed. "Yeah, a real great day. Get a few hours sleep, do some laundry, and come back to this place."

"But, Miss, it's a day. A day in your life."

She looked at the sun coming up, the stillness of early morning, the dew on the grass and flowers. "It is a beautiful day," she said to herself. And then in her thoughts, *Maybe I'll go to the park instead, and take a book.*

I stood on the steps and watched her go to her car. *I might take a rest today myself, but I'm gonna be back tonight,* I thought. I looked forward to cheering her up some more.

Back inside, they brung a little guy into Emergency. He cried and carried on like all get out. Had to keep my distance, so many people scurried around. But somehow I could see close up what was wrong.

"Little Jimmy," I said in my calmest shouting voice. Didn't want to scare the boy, but I did want him to hear me.

Jimmy cried and yelled and screamed something 'bout his insides coming out. He was a mess. I could tell that from down the hall. Truth be told, I didn't want to get closer for that reason. Didn't know if I could stomach it.

"Before we can help him," said a doctor, "we've got to get him sedated."

The boy tossed from side to side. A nurse struggled to give him a shot. "I can't get him still enough to give it."

An aide brought straps to hold him down.

His mama at his side didn't help much. "Jimmy," she cried out. "Oh my little baby."

From what I could see, the child was about the size of a ten-year-old, no baby at all. This mama had to see that her boy was growing up before her eyes.

None of what they're doing's helping things none, I thought. *Just getting him more riled up.*

So I called out in a singsong voice, "Little Jim-my."

Still upset, he did look around to see who made that fool singsong out of his name at a time like this.

"Oh, Jim-my," I called, not to scare him, just to get his attention. Course, he couldn't see me none, but he heared me, yes he did, from way out in the hallway. "Oh, Jimmy catch corn an' I don't care," I sung, "Jimmy catch corn an' I don't care."

Now the boy's looking around to see who's crazy enough to be singing in this mess of a sit-yation.

"Jimmy catch corn an' I don't caaaaarrre . . ." I held it a long time.

That little boy sat right up, all angry-like. "It's not 'catch,'" he shouted, "it's 'crack.'"

Right then, they got him good.

"Ow!" he cried, looking at the needle already coming back out of his arm.

". . . my master's gone away."

He was out like a light.

The other ghosts didn't like what I was doing.

One day, my nursie pushed a crash cart into a room. I followed, shouting, "Go to the Light! Go to the Light!" to a little gal ready to leave this old world, when a Shadow flew up in my face and got real big.

"SHUT UP!"

Scared the living daylights out of me. But the commotion going on in the room pulled at me. I had to help that girl. "OUTTA MY WAY," I said in the biggest voice I ever made. Was a good one too, though it didn't match his.

"All we want is a little PEACE AND QUIET!" he yelled and disappeared.

I turned to the little gal, who by now was near the ceiling. She looked at me, and I looked at her and said, "It's gonna be just fine. You wait a minute. They'll come get you."

And lickety-split, don't you know, she turned like somebody called her, and her face lit up just like that man I seen go before. "Mama!" she cried and vanished, just like that.

One big dark ghost like me—not a Shadow like me, a *Negro* like me—really hated what I was doing. "You're inSANE!" he shouted so loud the living heard it.

An old lady rolling by in a wheelchair turned to look at the boy pushing her down the hall. "What did you say?"

He was looking around too.

"Just SHUT UP!" yelled another ghost. This one was a Shadow—no doubting that—even darker than me.

Now all the folks in the hallway were looking at each other, shaking their heads, wondering if they were going round the bend.

I kept helping my nurse friend through, cause she could hear me real good. She said and even did some of the things I brought to her mind. And you know, these things I told her, sometimes I wondered myself where they came from, specially since I didn't know what I was talking about. But they seemed to work.

One day, I passed a room where a young man lay, his face and arms all bandaged up. "Burn victim," they called him. But who else did I see? One of our own—not a Shadow, a Cleary,

but a ghost even so—at his bedside, talking to him. I came a little closer to listen.

"It's gonna be all right," this ghost said.

I walked away smiling. We was helping.

Another time, a youngster ghost came up and said, "Hey,
Jeb"—they all knew my name—"there's a bad one over in
Emergency. Think you could help?"

We went down. A few tagged along to see what good a
ghost could do. Looking behind, I seen us all streaming to
Emergency.

We had us a team. Maybe we couldn't help our own selves,
but we could help others. *We're worth something*, I thought,
smiling.

I asked the young ghostling, "What's the problem?"

He shook his head. "Not sure. She's got plenty of family
around, on both sides."

He was right about that. Blue-eyed blondes with the
whitest skin ever packed the waiting room and hallway to the
trauma center. The Light from above showed the way, clear as
the Star of Bethlehem. We moved through the thick of the
crowd into the little cubicle. More blue-eyed blondes—from
the Other Side now—crowded round the bed so tight I
couldn't hardly get through, so I floated up to see.

There she was, her blond hair all straggly, dark blood
already crusting through a bandage wrapped round what might
have been a pretty face. Her left eye was swollen and bruised,
her teeth crooked and broke, and her little nose patched over
with another bandage.

A pretty young girl stood at the side of the bed. Looked to
be this one's twin, and I seen what the little hurt one should
have looked like—pretty hair all done up in bows, puckered
cherry-red lips, long eyelashes covering sad eyes.

She looked up as I hovered near the ceiling. Surprised, she
said, "How did you get up there?"

"Don't you know?" I asked. Then I realized the truth.

This little girl stood beside her own body, just like I had
stood next to mine when I died. I remembered how long it
took me to figure out I was really dead. She had so much to
learn.

"That's why I brought you here," whispered the ghostling next to me. We floated over to a corner. "She ain't leaving her body," he said. "I figure it's cause she don't know she can." He waved his arm. "She has all these people here to help her leave, and still she won't go."

I dropped down to the girl standing next to the bed. "Little girl," I said, then looked at the ghostling. "What's her name?"

He checked the chart on the end of her bed. "Josephine."

"Josephine," I said in her ear. "Girl, why you want to stay here like this?" I waved at her body all mangled and matted with blood. "You don't want this."

A tear slipped from her eye. I was getting through.

"Josephine," I said, "you ain't that little girl no more. Look at you!" I stood back and admired her neat trim little-girl self. She was a keeper. "You're so much prettier than that."

Her eyes moved to the pretty coat she wore in her "new" body.

"That's right," I said. "You ain't all tarnished and beat up like that body there."

Her eyes went back to the body in the bed. Her mouth turned down farther. Another tear slipped down her cheek.

I was wrong to bring her attention to the body she was leaving.

Now, you gots to realize, all this was going on in the middle of the hustle and bustle of nurses and doctors and aides and what-have-you running back and forth trying to keep her wasted body alive. We worked at counter-purposes, them and us, but there wasn't much hope of her having a good life if she stayed in that battered body. She needed to be free.

"Look, Josephine," said I, "you can stay in that body, but do you want to be crippled the rest of your life?"

She frowned.

"Look at it," I said. "They might be able to keep you alive, but do you want to be in a wheelchair till you die a second time?" Thought I might as well get the word out there.

A shriek from the waiting room, a rush through the door. The worst thing that could have happened at that moment, did. Her mama arrived and fell, crying and sobbing, on her little girl's body.

Josephine, the pretty one standing next to me, cried out, "Mama!" and leaned in for a hug, but of course her arms went through her mother. She jumped back.

"Now, now," I said, putting mine around her. "It's scary at first cause you don't know what's happening. But you with us now, Josephine. And look at all the loved ones you got waiting here."

Little Josephine wouldn't have none of it and cried and cried.

A large old woman pushed her way through the throng of relatives from the O.S. and tapped me on the shoulder. "I'll take care of this," she said.

Josephine looked up. Her eyes flashed. "Gran!" As she jumped into her grand-mammy's arms, beepers went off left and right. Nurses shoved the mama away and worked on the body to bring it back, but Josephine and Granny floated up and away, the crowd of welcomers leaving with them.

I watched till I couldn't see them no more. When I turned back, the room was clean, the bed made up, and everything back where it belonged, just as if none of this happened.

What a strange world we live in, I thought.

The ghostling gave me a wry look. We both smiled.

"*They* live in," I said, and floated out the door.

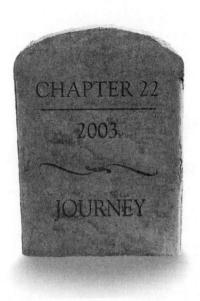

CHAPTER 22

2003

JOURNEY

Half the time we don't remember that we're ghosts, but those of us who do, look for a way to get through to the Living and get across to Heaven.
—J. Johnson

My nursie's name was Suz—funny name. One day, she was really down, so when it was time to go home, I followed her out and stayed with her all the way home.

"Cheer up," I told her, "it ain't so bad."

But Suz was what you'd call "blue." Her friends weren't well. They were dying, in fact. She had money problems, and the man rooming with her didn't pay his rent on time. He was supposed to help with the bills but sometimes didn't. Problems, she had problems.

As she drove along, she picked up the little phone piece y'all carry around now, punched the buttons, and waited. I heard the buzz as it rang on the other end.

"Hi!" she said, sounding chipper. Would have fooled anyone into thinking she was just fine. "Is your mom there?"

Listening to talks on the "phone" is different for ghosts. The other person's voice comes loud and clear through the listener's mind, so someone like me hears both sides of the conversation plus a few thoughts on this end.

This "mom" came on the phone. I supposed "mom" came from the word "mama."

"Hello?"

"Hi! It's Suz. How are ya?"

They chitchatted a while, sharing "what's new." Suz got down to her own problems and the mom shared her sympathy.

Then Suz asked, "How's the book coming?"

"Well, I sent the manuscript out to about twenty-five people," she said.

"You're kidding!"

"Just friends and relatives. You know, people who will honestly critique it."

"They know what happened?" asked Suz. "I mean about the ghost and everything?"

Ghost?

"Oh, yeah," the mom answered. "I don't know whether they believe it or not."

"Well, I believe it."

"You do?"

"Hell, yeah. You don't work around dying people all these years without seeing a few things yourself," said Suz.

"Well, it will be interesting to see what they think of the book," said the mom.

I gots to know this mom's name!

"So you put it all in there about helping the ghost and all?"

"Sure," she said.

She helped a ghost? Helped him what?

"I take the story all the way through his crossing."

I sat down. *She helped him* CROSS OVER? What did the Living know about such things?

The lady—*What is her name?*—sighed and said, "I just hope I can get it published."

Let me get this straight. This lady wrote a book about a ghost she helped get crossed over. Let me have that phone. Oh God, let me talk to this woman.

Then I remembered I wasn't helpless. I jumped up and yelled in Suz's ear: "HER NAME! SAY HER NAME!"

"Oh, don't worry, Linda," she said. "It'll get there."

"SAY HER LAST NAME!"

"You gonna use your own name? Or, you know, a pseudonym or something?"

"I thought about using 'Gloriana.' Remember when I got that name?"

"Yeah," said Suz. "Your dad thought you were disowning your heritage by not using your last name."

"In a way, he was right," she said.

Just say the damn name. . . .

"There's a lot of nobility in my last name. People in history, in education . . ."

"Gloriana's nice, too."

"Yes, and I believe that's my spiritual name, but I want to honor Dad. The only thing is, I'm not the only Linda Dewey around here."

Thank you!

"There's another one right here in Traverse City."

Where is Traverse City?

"And if there's another in Traverse City, think how many there are in the state. . . ."

What state?

". . . and in the country."

"So what are you gonna do?"

"I'll use my middle name," she said. "There can't be that many Linda Alice Dewey's in the world."

Jeb, I told myself, *you gots to get to that woman and sit on her doorstep till she helps* you.

"What's the weather like there?" asked Suz.

Where?

"Oh, you can see the islands," Linda answered. "The lake is pretty."

Islands. Water—a lake. *What lake?*

"You've sure been going through a bad time. You deserve something good to happen." Suz asked about the family and the broken marriage and this and that. All I wanted to know was where she was, where she was, *where she was!*

Finally, Suz said, "I might come up there."

Up? As in north?

"I've just got to get back to Michigan," said Suz.

Michigan. I remembered reading about the northern states back in little Miss Emily's storybooks. *Michigan.* I sort of knew where that was. Someplace in mid-something. I rubbed my hands together. *Now we're getting somewhere.*

"I've gotta get back there," Suz repeated. Her voice softened and I watched her eyes go dreamy. "It's so beautiful. I just love it. You've got the best spot, though, in Harbor Glen."

Linda Dewey in Harbor Glen, near Traverse City, in northern Michigan. In a flash, I was out the door.

I stuck my head back in.

Thanks, Suz!

And I was gone.

"Rest Stop 1 mile" said the sign as I flew overhead. Sounded good. I needed a rest.

I had to follow the highways—might get turned around if I didn't. Them signs along the way helped a heap. Without them, I didn't know where I was. I just knew that north was ahead if the sun rose on your right and set on your left.

I floated over to some parking spots and a little building where people went in and out and sat me down under a tree for a while. My God, I was tired.

When I woke up, it could have been hours later, could have been days. But it was the same season, so I knew it wasn't months. I sat and watched all the activity. Middle of the day, big square cars pulled in and dumped out passengers who walked to the "Welcome Center." Sometimes a beat-up old car full of young kids bellied up. Other times a big truck pulled in farther down and its driver took a few minutes to make a call or take a nap.

You didn't see really nice cars pull into these places. But as the day rolled on, there were fewer cars with families and more beat-up or souped-up jobs.

Now, I was plenty worn out, so I took my time doing just what "rest stops" were made for, but it wasn't hard to notice some of the funny business going on. Like the young adult types that came in all by their lonesomes and pulled in down a ways, just sitting there like they's minding their own business, when not too long after, another lone person—could be any age, really—pulled up next to the first. The second was almost always a man.

Then the fun began. Money changed hands for a little hoochie-coo of some sort. Lots of times it was drugs—I knew about drugs, oh yes indeedy—sometimes, something else. But then a lady would pull in, get out of her car, get into his, and off they'd go. A few hours later, back they'd come. She'd get back in her car, and both would skedaddle.

Nighttime was best. That's when the hanky-panky took place right in that parking lot. Sure, it happened in the daytime, but more at night. Whether it was male-female or male-male didn't matter. Nothing hardly ever went on inside the little building. Mainly, it happened in the cars and trucks. Hoo-boy, did it ever.

I wasn't the only ghost in this place either. Seemed to be a hangout for types of any kind looking for a place to go. Some, like me, even knew where they wanted to get to.

Best thing about these places is the maps inside—usually of the whole state and sometimes of the whole freeway—posted right up there on the wall. Them rest stops were a Godsend. They got me up to northern Michigan, but then the map said I had to get off the interstate.

Now there would be no rest stops with maps posted. How would I find the town of Harbor Glen? I floated above the cars. Linda lived in the northwest part of the state. I been traveling north all this time. Maybe now was the time to turn left and go west.

I thought about travelers that came to this place of pines and lakes and wondered where they stayed when they got here. Why, the answer was obvious. Hotels of course—motor hotels, or "motels" they called them now. Finding one by the road, I floated in behind a family of five loaded down with suitcases and what-have-you. They went up to a check-in desk, just like we used to in the old days.

I stayed around the desk. People almost always asked for directions. It was just a matter of time before I heard someone ask, "Can you tell us how to get to Harbor Glen?" By George, if they didn't get directions practically to her doorstep.

I followed that car all the way. Knew I was getting close by the number of ghosts walking alongside the road. They must have heard about her too.

We gather round people that might be able to hear us and can tell we're around. There ain't hardly a ghost that don't want somebody living to know he's there. We'll do all kinds of things to get your attention—slam-bang all night if we have to. Why at night? Well, how are you gonna hear us in the daytime with all that racket you folks make?

This must be the place, I said to myself. It was packed with ghosts. A small village, it was real pretty—good for tourists—sitting on big water that looked like an ocean. I roamed around, leery of socializing with other ghosts. But I did listen in on their thoughts and conversations.

"Sometimes," said a Cleary, "she goes into the woods over there." He pointed to the forest behind a restaurant. "The old cemetery where she found that Aaron ghost she helped cross is back in there."

"Nah," said another Cleary. "They can't do that."

"It's what they say where I come from." Seemed to be a down-to-earth sort, for a ghost.

"And where would that be?"

"What?" he asked back.

"Where ya come from!" This Cleary had a temper.

"I come from down south," he said, as he watched a family of Shadows on their way into the woods.

She looked at him different. "That's a mighty long way for a ghost to come, wouldn't you say? Don't people down that way help ghosts? Hear they talk to spirits all the time out there."

He nodded. "You hear a lot of talk. Some can. But this was a real crossing."

They watched ghosts here and there disappear into the brush.

"Every once in a while she visits the little cemetery in there."

She squinted, looking closer at the trees. "There's a cemetery in the woods?"

He nodded again. "Like I told you. An old one, no longer used."

"Anyone like us there?" she asked.

"You mean at the graves?"

She nodded.

He shook his head. "No, no. He was the last." He looked up. "But lots wait for her in the woods."

Worried now about competition, I surveyed the town. A grocery stood on the corner across from the restaurant. *She must go there every once in a while,* I thought, so I went in, found a comfortable place, and waited it out.

Sooner or later, I thought, *she'll show up.*

CHAPTER 23

2003

CONTACT

You don't really know who's gonna be the one to send you over.
—J. Johnson

People passed in and out through the store's swinging doors. It being an everyday place, people didn't mind their p's and q's like they did in a hospital. Lord, did I get an eyeful, an earful, and a headful of how people are nowadays. The cursing and complaining—even in a nice place like this with "gourmet" foods and all. Everybody was either honest, trustful, and naïve as hell—like there ain't nobody bad in their world—or just the opposite with a dingy, disgusted air about them—people who thought nobody was good cause *they* weren't.

When the cashier said how much they owed, people paid with a colorful little card that had raised letters and numbers. I got right up to see customers pass the card through a machine. How could cards be better than money?

I looked real close and seen why they were better than anything for me.

They had the customer's name on them.

Got so I could read them "charge cards" or "debit cards" or "bank cards" pretty good. I seen one with a "Linda" on it but not "Linda Dewey," so I didn't pay no attention. I should have, cause one day, this Linda bumped into a friend at the store.

"How's the book coming?" the friend asked.

I perked up.

"Oh, I sent it out to some friends a while ago to see what they think," Linda said.

"Really?" said the friend. "I'd like to see it."

Linda bought her groceries and headed out the door with me right behind. Soon as she got to her car, I started in.

"Linda!" I called. When she didn't answer, I yelled, "LINDA!!!"

We rode to her house, and she put away groceries while I jumped around trying to get her attention. All day I hounded her. Nothing worked. The house was quiet—no noisy music or TV going on. You'd think she'd have heard me.

She went into a little office and sat at a computer machine like at the hospital and typed letters and such. She even worked on her ghost story, rearranging this or that so it fit better.

I know. I listened to every thought. Hearing her read what happened to Aaron, I got caught up in it and, skipping ahead, read over her shoulder. She got to a really good part and shut the whole thing off to take a break.

"LINNNNDA," I called as she moved from room to room, straightening up. Over and over I tried. Finally, I sat down in the middle of the main room.

"Lady, why can't you hear me?" I asked as she rushed all around.

Lordy, I thought, *what am I gonna do?*

The back door opened. In walked a tall youth with dark blond hair, a pack slung over one shoulder. He went straight for the icebox, then grabbed a bag of something out of the cupboard and headed for the stairway. Never said hi, hello, or nothing. It wasn't a big house. He had to know she was there. He climbed the stairs, went into a room, and shut the door.

The house began to thump.

Linda got a broom and hit the ceiling with the broomstick. "Evan, turn that down," she shouted—her first words since coming home.

The thumping lessened.

"More," she yelled.

It lessened again.

Ain't nobody gonna hear me in all this noise, I thought and went outside for relief.

I sat under a tree and closed my eyes. This woman was what they call "oblivious." Picked that word up a long time ago cause it has truth in it. Lots of us are oblivious. Makes no matter if the sun's up or down, we all walk around in the dark.

I stayed for days, trying to get through and never gave up. And do you know why? Cause so many things got my hopes up.

One night, this little lady sung her heart out into one of them handheld deals that makes your voice loud. REAL loud.

"Let's roll, baby, roll,"

Song made no sense.

"We're going to the roadhouse and we're gonna have a reeeeeeeeeeeal . . . good time."

I thanked the Lord Almighty when she turned the machine off. Then she got all gussied up and went to her roadhouse, I guess.

I stayed behind to recuperate, but the worst was yet to come.

Now that a few years have passed and he's grown up some, I can see that her son's a good sort. But he was into mischief back then.

Linda no more than got down the road and lickety-split, he was downstairs taking over the music machinery. He put in a silver disc and this God-awful thumpity music shook the entire house.

It was everything I could do to stay inside. When I couldn't stand it no longer, I jumped in front of him and shouted, "TURN IT OFF!"

Watching his reflection in a big window that looked out on the black night, he never saw me.

"SHUT IT OFF!"

He bobbed up and down, arms all akimbo, making funny signs with his hands—as oblivious as his mama. When he moved into my space, I jumped to the side. Bouncing up and down with singsong talk, he looked my way—and saw me.

Not quite so sure of hisself now, he looked back at his reflection in the window, then over at me again.

My friends, this boy stopped and looked at me, then turned everything off, went upstairs, and closed his door tight.

The next day, he told Linda. "Mom, we're not alone. . . ."

"Oh, honey," she began, "of course we're not alone. God's all around . . ."

"No, Mom," he snapped. "We're not ALONE."

She stood there a minute, her thoughts reaching out to me. *If you're there,* she thought loud and clear, *talk to me.*

"Ma'am," I said, "I'm right here next to you. And do I have a story for you."

She rushed into her office and turned on her computer machine.

I followed her in.

Dear God, I heard her pray as the computer warmed up, *let me be clear.* The computer finished its shenanigans and she typed up what her son had just said.

Her voice came to me from her mind. *Are you there?*

I said aloud, "Yes, ma'am. I hear you. Take this all down, ma'am, take it all down."

So she did, and this is how she wrote it.

"I ask you to tell my story before I leave, cause I'm in no doubt I will be leaving shortly with your help." I told her about my earliest days, about my upbringing, and how Mama carried me on her back everywhere we went.

My mother did her best to bring me up but that was taken out of her hands when I was fourteen and had to go work in the fields. I was old at the time, for she had kept me from the work by making pretend I was helping at the house. What she really was doing was keeping me there so she could bring to me all the books the white children learned from, and together we pored over them till we had it right . . . or at least we thought we did.

I told her my story right up through that bad time after I left the militia.

I stopped. It was too hard. But she had a right to know what kind of man she was dealing with, didn't she?

So I told her.

I'll never forget what we did to that family.

You say my shadow your son saw last night was black, and now you're thinking it was black cause I'm a Negro, but that ain't the reason. A black man can have a white shimmer around him this side of the Crossing. Mine is black cause I am black—inside and out.

She wondered how I heard about her. Before she could even ask, I answered.

I heard about you from Suz and then from others. Word travels and so do we. When we hear about someone who passes us over like you did that one ghost, we come to be near you. We don't mean no harm, but I guess you can feel us, and if we ain't happy sorts, you take some of that on, don't you? You could ask us to leave, but we'd hang around outside your door. If that's not all right, we can go over to that cemetery where you found Aaron.

That's another way we know about you. Your book done already made the rounds over here. People where you are read it, and we read it over their shoulders or hear the words in their minds. This is a big way we know about you. Lots of ghosts seen this book now and talk about it.

I done traveled all the way from North Carolina to find you, Linda Alice Dewey.

If you like, till you cross me—and I know you can

do that—I'll stay outside. In fact, we'll all just go over
to the cemetery in the woods now—I think you like
that idea. We'll come back when you call us.

What's your name? she asked in her mind.

Never thought twice about it. She had to know the whole
story, and my crazy name was part of it.

"My name? It'd be Jacobs, ma'am. Jacobs Johnson."

Jacobs? she asked, like they all used to.

I smiled. "Yes ma'am, Jacobs with an *s.*"

You can tell me your story after you've crossed over, you know,
she said.

"Ma'am, my guess is there are too many waiting their
chance to do that. I figure I can get your attention better now."

She nodded.

"Then I'll go if it's all right with you, ma'am."

When will you be back? she asked.

"Soon again, at your behest, ma'am. But if you forget,
please don't mind if I remind you."

She smiled, thinking of how Aaron moved something to
get her attention, and then just a day ago how her son saw me.
I'd find a way.

Okay, she thought to me.

"Thank you, ma'am. I'll be leaving now."

Soon as I left, another ghost named "Daniells" took my
place, asking to tell his story. And wouldn't you know, she took
his down too.

Next morning, Linda sat down to that computer and said a
prayer like the night before. It was my time to shine. This is the
way she typed it out.

Thursday, September 25, 2003

Hello there, ma'am. Thanks for inviting me in. I
thought you might forget about me when you talked
to Daniells last night. But I see you keep your word,
and I'm right happy about that.

I won't be long in telling my story. I thought

about it, and you're right—we can add to it from the
Other Side. So many more here need to go over, it
wouldn't be right for me to take up all your time.

It would be good, when the time comes [for
crossing], if we invited the other ghosts in to see it.
Then they'll know for sure what happens. I did see it
the other night when you were with your friend and
helped them ghosts at the other house.

She paused, remembering how she helped a scared little
Cleary at her friend Cathy's house a few nights before.

Cathy had called on the phone. "I think there might be
someone here."

"You mean a ghost?"

"It just feels funny. The dogs aren't acting right. The cat
keeps looking at things that aren't here. At least *we* can't see
them," Cathy answered.

We all followed Linda as she drove into the woods and way
up the hill behind her house. She stopped in a long drive that
curved in front of a house and knocked on the door. Dogs
barked. Her friend came to the door and let them out. They
rushed at us, and we scampered away from the property. They
followed us to the end of the yard where the trees began and
never stopped barking.

Linda and Cathy stood on the porch, watching.
"*Something's* out there," said Linda.

Cathy called the dogs in and, when everybody went inside,
we snuck back to the house. After a while, a few of us went in.

Linda and Cathy walked through the house.

"I think I feel somebody in this bedroom." They lit candles, filling the room with a soft glow. Linda stood still for a
few minutes, her eyes closed.

The little one Linda felt watched from a corner. None of us
watching would forget seeing that little girl's face fill with rap-
ture just before she vanished into her Light.

"That was the first time you crossed one over by yourself,
wasn't it, ma'am?"

You know about her? Linda asked me now.

"Oh yes, ma'am," I answered. "Some of us even seen it. Everybody here knows what you been doing on your book and now this. Maybe one or two passings-on in between, but you ain't helped no other 'ghosts' except for her and Aaron, right?"

The "passings-on" were a few she helped leave that were dying but hanging on. Knowing it wouldn't do no good for them to stay, she found a way to talk with them in her head, like she did with me, and helped them see it was time to go. Each one passed a few hours later, instead of days or weeks or months. One lady had been hanging on death's doorstep for two whole years. Linda talked with her in her thoughts from two states away. Four hours later, she passed right over.

"Well, thank you for listening to me now. I'll get on with it then."

I told my story, but not every little thing like here in this book. Plus, I didn't know as much then. You learn a lot when you cross over and see things a mite different than when you're on the planet.

I did have a word to say at the end.

> I don't know if there's a God, or why He makes people like he does, or if they make themselves that way. Maybe I'll find out when I go over. But none of us is happy. There's not a happy ghost. But you give us the first hope we've had in a long time.
>
> Now, we know you can't help all of us. There have to be more people like you. But we have a feeling about you, that you're gonna make something happen where maybe others will learn through you. And maybe you can set it up so more go over at one time, like the Judgment Day, where they all go at once.

That last was one bad idea. When she tried it, folks got through that shouldn't have.

"I'm ready now if you are, and the ones Over There are ready to take me," I said. "Thank you for letting me have my say."

You're welcome, Jacobs, she thought back to me.

She printed out the pages and took them to her son, who was sick and home from school. He read it, then looked up at her. His eyes filled. Until then, he didn't really believe.

"It's him," he said. "I don't know how I know, but I do."

I got myself all ready for the Big Moment.

Linda looked at her son, seeing how he cared. "Why don't you sit with me. Let's see if there's anyone else here."

Now, ghosts had been streaming in all morning to see what was going on. Got so crowded, one of them made everybody line up to wait their turn, all nicey-nice and on their best behavior. That line went out the door. Don't know how I got to be first, but I thanked my stars I was.

Evan sat down next to her on the sofa. One of the others came forward. I kind of liked this lad, Daniells.

Evan spoke right up. "Somebody's standing beside me. It's Daniells."

Daniells told his story. When he finished, I stood straight and tall in the center of the room. Linda lit a candle and they both closed their eyes.

Then it happened. The ceiling opened and the sky overhead parted. I thought I seen a light and floated up into the separation without even trying—it just took me up with it. I tried looking ahead, but it was too bright for my old eyes, so I looked down at all the other ghosts looking up at me. Seeing me go was a magnet. They swarmed in from everywhere to watch. I smiled and waved goodbye.

The roof closed under me. I couldn't see Linda or Evan or the rest no more. Then the sky closed below, and I kept traveling with this light that wasn't so white and bright after all.

CHAPTER 24

2003

NOTHING

People think it ain't at all the way the Lord promised.
But you know, that ain't true. It's exactly what He said—
it just ain't the way you took it.
—J. Johnson

Floating in this greenish glow, I can't see anyone or anything of the world no more. Nothing—just this lime-green Space I'm in. I keep waiting, thinking surely somebody will come get me. Ain't that what they say—that everybody who loved you waits to welcome you over?

After a while though I give up, go into hibernation, and wake up later.

Am I really awake? I ask myself. *My crossing was real. But if it had been a dream, this is a worse nightmare, cause now I'm in a place I don't know.*

There's nothing to do, no place to go. There's no *place*, no time—only space.

I give up and go into my shell again. At some point, though, you gotta give up giving up.

All I got is me and my thoughts, me and my thoughts. There's nothing much I can do with me. Sure, I can move around and do wing-dings, but after a while that ain't no good cause it ain't changing things.

That's it. There's got to be a change.

I say aloud, "All right then. The only thing I got is my thoughts, so that's what I'll do—I'll think."

A thought shoots back from nowhere. *You got more than your thoughts.*

I straighten up. I just heard another voice. Sure, it was in my head, but it *was* another voice. Maybe somebody's talking at me in my thoughts, like I talked to people in theirs.

I answer back. "What else I got besides my thoughts?"

You got everything there is.

What kind of rubbish is this? "I got nothing," I say aloud.

You got more than nothing. You got your sanity.

"Sanity. What good is sanity?"

Course, now it's got me thinking. It would be worse if I was hallucinating. Then again, maybe this is just one big hallucination. Maybe life was just One Big Hallucination. Maybe I'm just like them people I seen in the hospital, all dazed and confused. But I don't feel dazed and confused. I can think straight.

You can *think straight.*

Like a man on a deserted island who sees he ain't alone, now I got something to bounce things off. But if nobody's here but me and myself, there's a bigger question. Am I splitting off into two people?

This ain't like that.

Aha! It said "ain't." Talks like me. Must be me.

Because we come through your mind, it sounds like you talk. We arrange words in ways like you say them. But we beg to differ.

I would never say that.

"Who's this 'we'?" I ask.

We are here to help.

"Oh, so I'm not alone then?"

You are never alone.

I look around. "I don't see nobody else here."

People on Earth think they're alone in a room, but you your-
self know that the room is full of spirits they can't see.

"So I can't see you, but I can hear you, like some can back
on Earth?"

That would be correct.

"See now, I don't talk like that. One minute you say 'ain't'
like me, and the next you use words like I don't say them. So
what kind of bullshit is this?"

This is . . .

They leave me alone, maybe cause I cussed and argued.

I say, "Hello? Hello? You out there?"

It don't answer, so I go back to my own thinking and
remember . . . something about Linda, the night she met—

I ain't told you this part yet. It was while I was trying to get
her attention. She was with her lady friends. She called it their
"Spiritual Listening Group" and . . .

Now, I'm telling you the God's truth, so don't close this
book cause you think this is going off the deep end.

That night in her little meeting with the other three ladies,
I seen Him with my own eyes. They couldn't see Him, but I
could. Knew who He was right away, and folks, if that ain't the
Second Coming, I don't know what is. He talked to them, and
they repeated to each other what they just heard Him say in
their minds, and I thought, *These women might not see what all's*
going on, but they know.

Come to think of it, I remember people at the chapel in the
hospital praying and talking with angels and Jesus and other
teachers and saints. Seemed like high beings from whatever
religion they believed in came to them and talked right back to
them too! Those people walked away feeling comforted, like
something happened in there. And it did, didn't it?

So now I ask myself, *Is this like that? Do I hear somebody*
real from another place that I just can't see?

I talk to that voice like I believe in it. "Are you part of me?"

It gives confusing answers. *You are never alone.*

"So are you here with me?"

We take care of our loved ones.

"Are you saying you love me?"

You are created by the Almighty One. Who are we to judge?

I look at myself here in this God-forsaken space and ask, *Well, if I'm not judged, why the hell am I here?*

Judgment is suspended, as are you, until you are free.

I laugh. "I spent my whole life looking for freedom. This is fitting."

Incorrect. You had energy bursts towards freedom, but you never became free.

"Well, whoever you are, I 'beg to differ.' I was after freedom." *Hmmm.* "But I never got there, you're saying?"

No.

All that traveling north from Alabama during the War never really got me free. I begin to see the truth. I wasn't after freedom. I was after "getting." Getting free, getting women, getting food, getting warm, getting outta there—getting, getting, getting.

Why did anyone put up with me? Then I see that, after a certain point, nobody really did. For women, being with me was just one step better than being alone. When it wasn't, they dumped me.

I do believe, though, that I redeemed myself somewhat in the Afterlife with my good deeds.

From then on, I have my talks with "them" and see what I done and what I didn't do. I see that, just like my twisted foot don't mean nothing here cause there's nothing to walk on, my twisted foot and my twisted self didn't mean nothing in life either. I could have helped folks out like I did later when I was a ghost. I was independent—free to help people, even in life. I just never knew it. I could have *done* something in life, instead of waiting for life to *happen* to me.

There's more to things than what's in front of our eyes— other ways to be besides living or dead. Oh, I don't know all the different ways there are of being. But I do know that we ain't here for nothing.

You are. Run with that.

That's all you need to know—and that there's more out there.

My hibernations now ain't like my earthly hibernations when I just conked out. This is more like dreams that have me going on adventures. They're so damn real, they seem like more than dreams. In some, I see Linda, her son, and her lady friends in her living room. In others, I talk in her ear like I used to with them cops.

She feels me near but thinks it's a ghost. "I can't help you," she says, shooing me away. "I'm not doing that work anymore."

What?

"I sent that first one up, that Shadow . . ."

You mean me?

"And then I sent tons up, banks of them at once like he suggested. But another ghost told me that it wreaked havoc on the Other Side. And that felt true."

Havoc? I think about my time so far in the Green Space. *You didn't send me to no havoc. Might not have been your Grand Crossing, but . . .*

"He told me that everybody had to run around over there and catch the ones I crossed prematurely. Somehow he knew. He said they even sequestered some to keep them separate, because they weren't ready." She sighs. "I didn't even know about Shadow People. Thought I was doing some good, lightening up this planet. But all I did was make extra work for them over there."

Sequestered?

She talks away. I float in and out of the woods across the highway but only see a few ghosts. There used to be so many. . . .

"So I stopped. I haven't crossed them over for a couple of years," she says.

Years? Lady, you helped me. Truly, you did. Might not be like most, but it helped.

I float alongside as she takes her daily constitutional up and down this highway that separates the land of the Living from a forest that used to be full of the Dead.

Let's say maybe you did cross some over "prematurely." Is that so bad?

"I hate making more work for everybody over there," she answers. "I'm not doing it anymore until I know how to do it the right way."

Ma'am, please don't stop.

But she does.

CHAPTER 25

2006

BRIGHTNESS

This work ain't for the faint of heart.
—J. Johnson

Oft times, I visit her in my dreams. Still, she won't help the few sad souls waiting around for her. They're even sadder now. The only thing they thought might work, ain't working.

I start feeling for them. Going up to one who can't see me, I pat him on the back and say, "It's gonna be all right. You'll see. There's hope." But he don't look no happier.

I plead for them, asking her to please go back to doing the work. So many lost souls wait to go over and, as far as they can see, there ain't no other way.

When you've only seen it done one way, you think that's the only way it can be done. But there's lots of ways to do things.

A friend of hers comes to stay. They go into little séances— no, no, "meditations."

In come some of them holy figures I told you about.

"Helping ghosts is needed Work," one says aloud.

Off in my corner, I think, *You bet it is.*

"But how can I tell who's ready to cross and who's not?" she asks them.

"You'll know."

"I didn't know before. What's different now?"

"You'll just know."

Another time she's walking down her road real fast, kicking up a storm.

"God," she prays, "if you want me to do the Work, give me a way to know which ghosts are ready and which aren't."

Ghosts seep out of the woods and trail her down the road. They crowd in, trying to get close so she'll feel them with her.

"Linda," I yell, "tell them to come to you one at a time."

She does.

One comes up to her, alone, and she does something new.

"Put your hand on my shoulder," she says to this first one. They walk together, his ugly arm across her shoulder. Linda looks straight ahead. He watches her, waiting for the word.

Then she does it. "This one may cross over," she says. She thinks about over there on the O.S. "Let there be healers and loved ones waiting on the Other Side to help this one in its transition."

Up it goes, giggling and waving at the rest of us below. Then it turns to those waiting high above in the Light and disappears.

Makes me think of my own crossing. I want what he just got—folks waiting to welcome me, loved ones like Mama and my sister and brothers. They should have been at my crossing.

Maybe I didn't deserve it. I was, after all, a Shadow. Clearies don't have as much bad around them as we do. And why? Why was I a Shadow, anyway?

Maybe cause I was a robber, a stealer, a liar, and a cheater. Maybe cause I never thought I could do no good and, after my little shot at teaching, gave up and took whatever life dished out. Maybe cause I didn't speak up when I should have, when I could have stopped something bad going on, right back to that family in the farmhouse and even before that.

Maybe cause I didn't believe in myself, really. Ever. Maybe that's why I deserved what I got. And didn't get.

Was I still like that?

Back on the road, the others get so excited they forget their single-file line and rush to be next.

"Back off!" she yells. "I can't tell who is who if you crowd me."

Good girl! Show 'em what you got!

Angels, she prays, *I need a Gate Keeper.*

Moving in, I walk beside her and block the others till she's ready.

"Next," she says.

I let a little girl through.

"Put your arm around my waist." It takes a minute for her to feel this one's energy, then she crosses it over. Goes on like that for a bit, till a big burly guy pushes his way to the front. I don't like him, but it ain't up to me.

"Next," she says.

I let him through. He puts his arm on her shoulder and right away, she looks sickly and says, "I'm sorry, this one is not ready to cross over yet."

"Not ready?" he cries. "What the hell you talking about?"

"Time to go, man," I say, but he ain't budging.

"Please back away from me so I can help the next one," she pleads, but he ain't going no place. "I can't do this work with you around." She's as green as my Green Space.

Meanwhile, I'm a-tugging and he's throwing me off. We're about to get into it good when she casts her eyes upwards.

"Angels, please remove this one."

Now, ghosts don't usually see angels. I never did and never talked to any that did. Didn't know they existed. So as far as this guy's concerned, a big wind nobody else feels up and pushes him into the woods.

But me, I see who done it. An angel, big and fierce with a sword and scabbard and feathery wings, pulls that guy right outta there. Stops me in my tracks. Without a word, the angel is gone.

After a while, I dream more and wake up less and less in that Green Space. Linda and I meet up lots of times on her daily walks.

Miss, you gots good work ahead, helping them ghosts. They's all around, you know, waiting patient-like.

"Are there any ghosts here that need help?" she asks, and they sidle on over.

I check around. Them backwoods is full of them again. Makes me happy to see business back to usual.

Still, though, the minutes tick away while she's close with a ghost, till she can tell who's ready to go and who ain't. Sometimes, when one is nearby that ain't ready, she'll get a headache or feel sickly. Seems to me that doing something good shouldn't make a person sick.

In my Green Space time, I have questions on how to help her better in my dreams.

It's all in the intention, they tell me.

"What you mean, 'intention'?"

Your motivation. What do you wish to do when you visit her?

"She helped me. I figure it's only right to help her back, even if it's only in my dreams."

And so it shall be.

I get to help more and more. Sometimes I tell her this one ain't ready, or that one's still a Shadow, and she gets better and better at feeling the difference between Clearies that are ready to go and them that ain't.

One day, though, there's something different in how she goes about it.

My scalp tingles, she says inside herself. *Someone's here.*

Sure enough, one comes out of the woods. She bids it to come close, then stops.

"The skin on my leg! It's like there's silk sliding on it." The hairs on her arm stand straight up. "My skin is crawling!" She dances—arms held out, twirling in the sunlight. "Everyone talks about their skin crawling or their hair standing on end. Mine's finally doing it too!"

She done prayed and prayed for a better way to know they was near, and now she has it. She don't have to "tune in" to see if they're around—the tingling and crawling tell her one's close. She ain't felt the cold that gets to your heart when one comes by. Not yet. But the touch, she's got.

That day she crosses them one after another.

Lord Almighty, this woman has come a long way! I think. *Yes, she has.*

I'm learning too and look up at the beautiful blue sky that's so bright, I have to squint. I do believe it's the brightest sky I seen since dying. Looking back down at myself, I see why.

I ain't dark like I been. I stretch out my arm. *The shadow's gone!* No wonder the sky's so bright! And the trees! And the flowers! And . . . everything! *Oh, what beautiful colors.* I ain't seen things this clear since . . . maybe forever!

"Your shadow is gone," says the Green Space voice, "because you choose silence no longer when you can help and make a difference."

I think back to the day I helped little Sherilee—how the sky seemed bluer then—and wonder if this happened slow since then, so gradual I didn't even notice—till now!

Then I see the biggest change of all. Didn't notice before cause I glide now instead of walk. But, looking down—my bad old foot, it . . . it's just like my other. The twist is gone!

"Your twist is gone inside as well as out. You have made this so."

Glory, hallelujah! This IS a miracle! No shadow and that nasty old twist gone! Now I'm the one dancing in the sunlight, hopping and skipping and prancing along with both feets on the ground. I'm a happy man—oh yes, I am.

Then there's the day she walks along and nobody creeps up from behind, but still she starts to look around.

"Someone's here," she says, but there ain't nobody. "Come close," she says, but nothing happens. "Come on, it won't hurt."

Makes me sad. She thinks there's a ghost, but ain't nobody here 'cept for . . .

I move up a little.

"Closer," she says.

Aw now, lady, I ain't no ghost. But I move up a little more, just to keep her happy.

"Put your hand on my shoulder."

Jesus Christ Almighty. "Lady, you already done crossed me over!" *Lordy! She thinks I'm a ghost.*

She stops. "Put both hands on my shoulders."

She all mixed up, I think, but do it anyway.

Mixed up or not, here we stand. She looks off. By now, she can tell pretty good who's ready and who ain't. She tells the dark ones not to even bother.

So here I am, right up against her even though I'm not a ghost. But in this, uh, dream, I guess I must be, cause she says, "This one may cross over."

And lo, the Light! It's so damn bright! And it's mine. It's here just for me.

I float up and this time, why, they're all here—Mama and my sister and brothers. And Papa! *Oh my God, Papa!* And there's Reynolds! The angels are here, and He's here too, and hooded men and what look like they're maybe rabbis. So many a-waiting just for me! I clasp each one's hand like I ain't gonna let go, till I see another and move to that one. Mr. Tate! Ha! I start to laugh, and everybody's so full of smiles, they laugh too.

I look back, but Linda's gone, and the street and woods and everything of that world is gone too.

Hallelujah! I done crossed over for real!

"So," says someone behind me.

I'd know that voice anywhere.

"I see you learned about 'intention.'"

I turn around to see a tallish man with dark hair and clear blue eyes dressed in coveralls.

"I've been working with you from This Side." He steps forward and offers his hand. "Name's Aaron."

We shake for a long, long time cause I can't say nothing.

Then something troubles me. "So that Green Space . . . was that a dream?"

He smiles. "Just a temporary reality."

"And coming to help Linda . . ."

"Another reality that brought you here. Which one was the dream?" He shrugs. "Maybe neither." Smiling, he watches me try to make sense of it. "Don't worry. Your Green Space time is through."

Relief washes through me. But then I notice something else. "You don't sound . . . but . . . I heard you were Irish."

He laughs. "Irish?" He shakes his head. "Ireland is where I was born—there. But here, we come from a far earlier place

before we live on Earth. When we return, we're back the way
we used to be."

"But you look like Aaron might," I say, noting his farmer's
coveralls and the dark hair.

"Just so you'll recognize me." With that, he changes into a
lovely young woman.

I gasp.

She laughs and changes into a little redheaded girl.

I jump back, and he quickly changes back into Aaron.

"We're many aspects rolled into one. That's the beauty of
it. We can be whoever we want."

"And I chose to be a runaway slave with a twisted foot. . . ."

"And look where it got you!" says Aaron, noting all who
came to see my return. Old Mammy, blind old Horace who
ain't blind no more . . . even Jessie, from that field! The old guy
whose pocket was being picked that time. Little Sherilee and
the man who saved her from that stalker! Why, there are the
nuns! Everyone's here!

"Look who you helped, Jacobs, just by being who you are.
And look who helped you."

My eyes spill over just like my heart. All these people. I did
do some good after all, didn't I?

Over time, I been learning to help ghosts too. Lots of us
help Linda and anybody else doing this Work.

One day, I return. It's so different, coming from Over
Here, to see how things are for these folks. She's on her highway. I walk beside her again.

"I feel an angel chill," she says.

Now, I ain't no angel. No sirree Bob. Never will be, I don't
think. But I'm helping her do the Work. That I am.

Except this time, I've come just for me. I gotta do one
more thing.

"Ma'am," I say, as we walk along.

She does look like she's listening.

"Thank you for helping me, ma'am. Thank you from the bottom of my heart."

As I rise and float away, she's a-walking down that road, a little smile on her face.

EPILOGUE

AUTHOR'S
JOURNAL

Three years after Jacobs's crossing, I wondered if Jacobs, now on the Other Side, thought about us back here on this old planet. In our first communication since his crossing, I typed his words as I heard them with my inner ear. What he said became the source for the passages beginning each chapter. The following is his complete message.

May 16, 2006

I feel I owe it to those left behind to let you know what's what when you get here, and how you get here, and what you got to look forward to if you don't tend to yourself where you are right now.

You call it living, but to us, existing the way most of you do is death warmed over, nothing more. There's a lot more to life, if you want to live it. Or, you can let yourselves go stagnant and have the living death. I saw enough [of that] to last me three lifetimes while I awaited this lady's coming.

That's another thing—the Coming. You gots to
be ready and waiting, that's for sure, but you don't
really know who will be the one to send you over. It
will come. Just don't think you know how it's gonna
happen, cause for everybody it's different. Maybe it's
Him in disguise, wearing another face or coming
through one of his servants. Or maybe He'll come a
second time in a way you don't expect, like in your
dreams or a vision.

People think they got it all figured out. Then
something comes and riles them up, changing everything, and it ain't at all the way the Lord "promised."
But you know, that ain't true. It's exactly what He
said, just not the way they took it. That'd be the only
difference.

The Path appears in a way for you that just
couldn't be for no other. There is a time for you and
for me and for all God's children, cause there is a God.
Yes indeedy, never doubt that. He's there, a-sittin' and
a-waitin' for the moment when you finally see that
yes, it's His world, His game. When you admit that,
He's there for you in disguise, ready to help you cross
to the Promised Land. That's true for every one of us.

And you don't have to die to get there.

So don't be downhearted. It's all happening just
the way it needs to. You're each on the Path, that's
for sure. Stay true to yourself, yes, yourselves, to each
other, and to your God and none other. You'll see it
all come to pass, just like the Good Book says, but in
a way you'd never expect. Just watch and be alert,
cause you could miss it if you're not awake.

May 17, 2006

You wonder why this story is different from the
parts you wrote three years ago fore I crossed. I tell
you now, it isn't. Oh, you might get the names and
places a little mixed up, but you hear us darn rightly.

Oh, ma'am, you have no idea what's about to come out of this story, now do you? I can't speak for what you might learn, but I myself learned so many precious things—details some—but nothing is small when you look at it close enough, is it? Everything points to something bigger.

Just know that I am the same person what came to you that day. If I'm different, it would be cause I been here a good three years now and see things a little different than before.

Others wait here to tell their stories so people can know what happens. You would not believe what's in store. The angels have stories to tell too. I will tell what it's like, so I can help you understand the Work you do. I guess I'll start where I heared about you.

I heared about this woman Up North who helped a ghost. Big to-do over here, cause there ain't many on your side doing that kind of work. Most are scared of us. But all we do is just go about our own business—spirits still living lives. See, we don't remember half the time that we are ghosts. But those of us who do know, and I knew what I was—yes, indeed, I knew what I was when I was living and when I was dead—those of us who do know, look for a way to get through to one side or to the other. We look to break through to the Living and we look to get across to Heaven, 'cept most of us don't believe in Heaven cause we're stuck down there in a place we can't get out of.

That's the definition of hell—to be stuck, and nothing you do makes a difference.

When you're living, sometimes you think nothing you do matters, but that ain't true. As long as you're living, you can make a difference. As a ghost, though, it's hard to affect anything. The living don't know you're there, so they ignore even the big breakthroughs, unless a real powerful ghost wreaks havoc. Then all hell breaks loose. Most of us don't have that kind of power, though.

December 31, 2006

I'd been typing along, taking dictation: *"Ghosts—that's what we were, of course—came and went with this group. Shadows of souls—encased in our despair, our misperceptions . . ."* I began to doubt the veracity of a runaway slave using such terms.

These big words bothering you, ma'am? I'm not the soul I was, no ma'am. In fact, there ain't no color here, no country of origin, and I done linked up with my Super-Soul, if you want to call it that. I'm identifying with my life as Jacobs cause that's how I came to be with you, ma'am. But I'm so much more than that.

I do have someone by my side helping me relate these goings-on. It's not your Aaron. He's moved up in the ranks, so to speak.

We was Shadows, ma'am. The shadow surrounding each of us—our conflict, confusion, despair, guilt, shame, you name it—became visible when we died. Each person has his own shadow side and usually gets the better of it. Most of the time you can hide it, but for those of us who succumb, it becomes visible the minute you die.

Every ghost has problems, the biggest one being getting across to the Other Side. But it's more than that. Shadows have a hell of a lot of work to do before we can cross.

And yes, ma'am, you crossed me too early. It should have taken a whole lot longer for me to get over there, and you did make a whole lot of work for them on the Other Side. But they saw this coming and had a space ready for me. Oh, yes ma'am, they sure did.

At one point, I needed to understand more about the Shadows. This is the way he explained it:

Funny how once I was with them [the Shadows], we all began to have the same reactions. But there's more to it than that. You got to keep an eye out where you are too. Don't let yourself be mind-controlled by group thought. Takes away your individuality. You find yourself in agreement on small things first, then on big things, then pretty soon you're all the same.

At first with the Shadows, I just let them take the reins, cause I didn't think I knew anything.

In fact, if I were to say now why I was a ghost at all—especially a Shadow—I'd have to say it was cause of just that. I let others take over. I let life take over and didn't do nothing to stop it. There's things you can change and things you can't. I just never tried. All I wanted to do was just get through it. Never tried to do more. Never tried to be more. Never tried. I just let life slide by the same as I did with the Shadows.

A Shadow's light is hidden by a miasma of thought that creates a haze—a cloud—that partially hides the light, but not all of it. Makes it hard to see the real being and difficult for the being to see the real world.

My own false perceptions were about what life was for. I didn't know life was for getting to be a better person. I just thought it was about surviving. Silly, cause no one survives.

I did what I had to with the bookkeeper but could have used those skills further. Things went well until that school came into the community, then it all went downhill and I didn't see the point in being more, in "letting my light shine," like they say in church. I didn't see that I could do that. I just figured, "That's it for me," and went downhill from there.

I didn't hate no one but didn't love nobody either. I was there just to get through it. One way to do that was to make myself friendly with the ladies. I thought they was my survival tool. If I could hitch onto one of them, things might work out and I'd have a place to live. I never did make a place for nobody, not even for myself.

I used life, but never made use of life. That's the problem.

February 22, 2008

Finally, a few thoughts for you, the reader, from me. The first ghost I ever assisted was Aaron. In *Aaron's Crossing: An Inspiring True Ghost Story*, I explain how I became involved in this work because of that experience. Now I give three-hour workshops on how to help ghosts. A detailed manual would be another whole book, but I'll share some thoughts here.

When ghosts find out that a person may be able to help them, they come flocking. But they also learn to respect boundaries. If they don't respect mine and try to push my limits, they're obviously not ready to cross, and I tell them so. Then I ask the angels to take them away, and forget about it.

I've learned not to engage ghosts in conversation, especially if they're angry, argumentative, or pushy. I simply ask that they be removed. After that, I trust the situation is being taken care of and I certainly don't think about them. They're parasitic, and thinking about them gives them energy. If I don't pay attention to them, they'll leave one way or another. Sometimes an intuitive reiki or massage therapist removes any who are still attached to me. And I never do ghost work in my, or anyone else's, home.

When mourning relatives meet with me, it's not uncommon for a recently deceased ghost to join our meeting. A catharsis, usually involving forgiveness, may occur and the ghost crosses over. If the ghost is not ready, nothing can be done but help guide it with words of hope and, with a prayer, send it off with the angels for help.

Often when a ghost crosses, a chill begins at my feet and travels up and out through my scalp (crown). At book signings and lectures, I'll feel the ghost of a loved one near someone. Later, I'll talk with the person about it privately. Once the ghost hears it is forgiven, it may spontaneously cross. Accounts written by people who have experienced this with me can be found on the Forum at www.lindaalicedewey.com.

I was present at a car accident and intuitively knew someone had died, so I helped them cross. The wonderful, telltale, shimmer-shiver I feel when someone crosses told me when it happened and that it was all right. Later, I heard on the news that someone did indeed die in that crash.

Recently, I received an e-mail from a woman whose grandfather studied with the noted medium and psychic Jean Dixon. This woman said that the descriptions in *Aaron's Crossing* of the crossing-over process was presented exactly as her grandfather had taught her. Understand, my process of writing comes from telepathic listening. For someone who comes from adolescent insecurity, letters like these are not only heartwarming, they are absolute validation of our inner truth, intuition, and wisdom.

One of the first people to read *Aaron's Crossing* wrote that she was in tears for the second half of the book. She had grown up in a house inhabited by a ghost. Aaron's story explained so much of what had happened in her house, that it all finally made sense.

This is truly amazing work.

I no longer take down a ghost's story before it has crossed over. Too many need help getting across for me to take their stories down beforehand. There's plenty of time for storytelling once they're settled on the Other Side. Plus, isn't it wonderful to get the perspective from someone who has crossed and sees the broader picture?

Finally, these wonderful ghost-beings help me hone my intuition and trust my instincts. Through plenty of practice, they've taught me the value of standing firm in my truth with them.

I'm not the only person doing this work. Though not for everyone, many do serve in this capacity. Perhaps you are one who can do this too. Just don't do like I did and jump into it with great intentions before you know what you're doing!

The point is, in my case, all of this has been learned, which means others can and are learning to do this too. Do you find this kind of work intriguing? When something fascinates you, a gift may be calling. I was always fascinated by the spiritual, whether Bible stories or Jean Dixon. Never in my life did I think that one day I'd be doing this. But that love of "ESP" was a gift calling to me.

If you find yourself fascinated too, listen to that gift. See where it leads you. Learn what you can from others, but most of all, listen inside.

Jacobs's story is one of freedom—its resulting power, choices, and responsibilities. Jacobs felt he did not take his power when he could have, learned from his mistakes, and moved on.

I challenge you to examine the spiritual power that awaits each of us.

Find a way to harness yours.

Ride your way to Freedom.

About the Author

Linda Alice Dewey was born to a family with a metaphysical belief system that taught her "there are no such things as ghosts." But in 1987, she discovered a different sort of metaphysics and commenced a new spiritual journey that developed her spiritual skills. These include high spiritual listening or channeling, mediumship, psychometry, face reading, and general readings.

An award-winning writer and composer in school, Dewey taught public school for nearly twenty years. She's been a guest writer for local newspapers and on the staff of AbsoluteWrite.com. In the 1980s, Dewey wrote and produced music jingles for radio and television in Michigan and Arizona. No stranger to the stage, she's been in musical and theatrical productions all her life. A versatile singer, she continues to perform. Her paintings hang in homes across the country.

Linda teaches metaphysical workshops and a workshop on book promotion. Current writing projects include adapting *Aaron's Crossing* to the stage in a *Phantom*-like musical with original music. In addition, she continues her late father's work—a compilation of a twenty-year archive of documents about the Kassel Mission, a World War II battle which resulted in the greatest loss in a single day's battle by a group from a single air base. She is president of the nonprofit Kassel Mission Historical Society (http://kasselmission.com).

Dewey resides in northern Michigan in the cottage where Jacobs first contacted her, just a mile from the wooded cemetery where she first encountered the ghost of Aaron Burke. She has two grown sons and a daughter-in-law. You may write to her or comment on her Message Board/Forum at:

http://lindaalicedewey.com

Hampton Roads Publishing Company

. . . for the evolving human spirit

Hampton Roads Publishing Company
publishes books on a variety of subjects,
including spirituality, health, and other
related topics.

For a copy of our latest trade catalog,
call toll-free, 800-766-8009,
or send your name and address to:

Hampton Roads Publishing Company, Inc.
1125 Stoney Ridge Road
Charlottesville, VA 22902
E-mail: hrpc@hrpub.com
Internet: www.hrpub.com